Deepening Zen

Book Two

Mitra Bishop
Roshi of Mountain Gate Sanmonji, New Mexico, USA

Foreword by
Daishin Patrick Vigil

Introduction by
Jan Chozen Bays

Deepening Zen
Book Two
Mitra Bishop Roshi

Published by **Sumeru Press Inc.**
PO Box 75, Manotick Main Post Office,
Manotick, ON, Canada K4M 1A2

© **Mountain Gate** 124 County Rd 73, Ojo Sarco, NM 87521

Design and cover art: Genshin Jeremy Cranford

All rights reserved. No part of this book may be reproduced in any form or by any means, electronic or mechanical, including photocopying, recording or by any information storage or retrieval system without permission in writing from the author.

All efforts have been made to obtain copyright permissions from publishers and authors quoted in this publication. While many individuals have contributed to this book, unintentional errors and omissions are mine alone.

ISBN: 978-1-998248-04-9   ISBN: 978-1-998248-05-6 (Ebook)

Library and Archives Canada Cataloguing in Publication

Title: Deepening Zen. Book two / Mitra Bishop (Roshi of Mountain Gate Sanmonji, New Mexico, USA) ; foreword by Daishin Patrick Vigil ; introduction by Jan Chozen Bays.
Names: Bishop, Mitra, author.
Description: Includes bibliographical references.
Identifiers: Canadiana 20240464907 | ISBN 9781998248049 (softcover)
Subjects: LCSH: Dharma (Buddhism) | LCSH: Zen Buddhism.
Classification: LCC BQ9266 .B573 2024 | DDC 294.3/927—dc23

 For further information about The Sumeru Press, please visit us at **sumeru-books.com**

Dedicated to all who yearn for spiritual depth,
regardless of religious affiliation,
and to all who came before and showed the Way.

Contents

Foreword 7
Introduction 9
Preface 13

1. Foundations of the Deepest Zen Practice 17
2. When Anxiety Comes Up in Zen Practice 27
3. The Challenge of Letting Go 39
4. Escape Is Not a Solution 51
5. Jump into the 86 Hells 63
6. Zen Practice and Suppression of Feelings 77
7. Unweaving the Tapestry, Exploring the Mind 87
8. Benefits of Being Honed by Life and Zen Practice 97
9. A Story of Transformation: ACES and Zen 105
10. Struggle and Transformation in Spiritual Practice ... 113
11. Luminous Transparency and the Rapids of Life 121
12. Nirvana 129
13. A Featureless Map of Zen Practice 137
14. A Sufi Teaching Story 149
15. Fruits of Advanced Zen Practice 157
16. Post Sesshin Advice 173
17. Sensing Your Way Deeper Without a GPS 183

Glossary 195
Glossary of Kanji Translations 201
Recommended Reading 203
About the Author 207

Foreword

FREEDOM.

That word is commonly bandied about in American society. Each of us defines freedom differently, and to demonstrate our freedom we act and react in line with our personal thoughts and concepts. However, in acting out our thoughts and concepts we instead become trapped in the exact opposite condition. We become slaves to our concepts and end up being in a prison of our own creation. Our words and concepts bind us, not release us, and they have nothing to do with reality, as it is. This is not freedom.

Around 2500 years ago a deeply troubled man sat down under a tree and vowed not to get up until he found the path to liberation. Through that realization, that man became known as the Buddha and his teachings have been passed down over the course of millennia.

Mitra Bishop, Roshi, has for over 50 years incorporated and practiced those deep teachings in every aspect of her life. She lives each moment in true freedom. Roshi has crafted her messages and teachings with an eye to modern Americans, ordinary people who, like you and me, seek answers to our deepest questions. In examining and putting into practice her teachings, offered both in this book and her first volume, you will find your answers and a true path to ultimate liberation. As Roshi says "You will become increasingly free, and there is no end to the depths of that freedom." And this is her wonderful promise to each of us.

We invite you to walk the path and to incorporate these practices and teachings into your daily life.

Daishin Patrick Vigil

Introduction

This book is important. It is the second in a collection of Dharma talks by Zen teacher Mitra Bishop. Her voice is one of clarity and certainty made possible by her many decades of experience as a Zen student and teacher. The theme of these talks is the oft-overlooked need for long maturation, practice that continues to transform our life after initial openings into Original Mind. This unending practice infuses our entire life and gradually transforms our experience as an isolated human being living in a world of conflict and distress. Over time it reveals our true heart/mind, a reliable source of wisdom, loving kindness, equanimity and inner peace.

Buddhist practice rests upon experience, not blind belief. Mitra Roshi has done, and continues to do, the work of the long maturation. She has been practicing for 50 years (at least in this lifetime) and is able to share her wisdom about potential pitfalls along the path. This book will be helpful to all earnest Zen practitioners, as well as to students of the Theravada and the Vajrayana. I plan to include it in the readings we do each morning at breakfast at the Zen monastery where I live and teach.

As Zen has become popular, it has become commodified, used to advertise everything from antique stores ("Zen and Now") to "Zen T shirts" with messages including "I love Zen", " Zen AF" and "Hurry Up Inner Peace I Don't Have All Day." Long-term dedicated Buddhist practice has been trivialized into a "delicatessen approach," a collection of brief samplings such as an empowerment ceremony with a Tibetan guru, a weekend mindfulness retreat, ten days at a Zen monastery, a dark retreat in Guatemala, and an ayahuasca adventure with a shaman in Peru.

The Buddha taught that there is a path out of our suffering. Collecting Buddhist merit badges is not that path. The path includes long-term dedicated practice, an ever-deepening and ever-widening view and the seamless integration of transforming insights into all the activities of daily life. These are the themes of this book.

No one would expect to become an accomplished pianist after a few months of practice. But people (even, as Bishop recounts, the young Shodo Harada Roshi) do come to Zen practice with an expectation that they will have an enlightenment experience after a few months of meditation. When it doesn't happen on their anticipated schedule, they abandon practice.

Thank goodness that Harada Roshi returned to Shofukuji monastery, dedicated all his energy to clarifying the Great Matter of birth and death, and then devoted his life to guiding his many students, Mitra Roshi and myself among them.

When my root Zen teacher, Maezumi Roshi, came to the West, he was propelled by a vow. His purpose was "to plant the root of the Dharma so deeply in the West that it can never die out." He taught us to love and respect the power of zazen meditation and to submit to the penetrating and clarifying force of sesshin (seven to ten day silent retreats). We experienced that love and power for ourselves as we practiced zazen and sesshin. We experienced it in our daily lives, as freedom from the suffering caused by the mind's incessant weaving of the illusion of a separate, lonely, impoverished and inadequate/flawed self. When we were able to see through that illusion, life became a most interesting adventure.

As the 13th century Zen Master Dogen wrote:

> To study the Buddha Way is to study the self.
> To study the self is to forget the self.
> To forget the self is to be enlightened by the ten
>   thousand things.
> To be enlightened by the ten thousand things is to
>   drop off body and mind and the body and mind
>   of others.
> No trace of enlightenment remains and this traceless
>   enlightenment continues forever.

This is the most precious gift, the gift of a practice and a path that enables us to lessen and ultimately end our own suffering. Underlying

INTRODUCTION

all suffering is fear. I can write this here, but, as the Buddha said, "Don't believe it just because this old monk said it." Buddhism is not a religion of blind belief, but a practice of investigation, discovery, insight and joy. We test and confirm it through our own experience.

When we began Zen practice in the 70's we naively believed that a *kensho* opening would solve all our problems. We hoped, as Mitra Roshi writes, that we would be "...diving to the bottom and bypassing the psychological debris." She wisely encourages enlisting the help of psychotherapy when the debris blocks our path to freedom, when the strategies that helped us navigate difficulties in our life become stubborn obstacles to deepening our practice.

In several chapters she describes phenomena that often emerge as practice is sustained, phenomena that can derail us from continuing to deepen our understanding. One of these is anxiety. Our mind seems to believe that unless it is talking to us continually, warning us, criticizing us, reviewing our past mistakes or compulsively planning our future, we will come to harm and possibly die. As our mind quiets down in sustained meditation, the fundamental anxieties that underlies this tangle of thoughts can come to the fore. "What will happen to us without the mind's continual chattering? Who will we be if we aren't our thoughts?"

Another phenomenon Mitra Roshi calls "standing at the precipice." We feel that we are standing at the edge of the unknown and are unable to take the next step. This occurs when "the part of us that fears becoming truly free" throws up obstacles. A third phenomenon is "ego backlash," a common occurrence after a deep sesshin. The constructed self tries to take back its territory, often through inner criticism. Knowing about these phenomena helps us to remain steady and continue with our practice. A skilled and experienced teacher can guide us through them.

Bishop sprinkles her talks with lively Zen stories both ancient and modern, classic poetry, a lovely Sufi story, research on what enables people to transform themselves, and vivid personal accounts from her own life and the lives of her teachers.

Some of Mitra Roshi's pithy statements are koans in themselves and can become catalysts for ongoing investigation. Here are a few or my favorites:

> Suffering is caused by an attachment to a person and an attachment to a result. If neither of these exist, there's nothing to cause suffering.
>
> That luminous transparency is always there, beneath it all. We can open to it.
>
> The experience of kensho comes with an expanding sense of freedom, but unless the work of long maturation is ongoing that sense of freedom will fail.
>
> One kensho is not enough. We have to practice until it becomes a natural way of living.
>
> The work of long maturation becomes joyful as time goes by.
>
> There is no shortcut to long maturation.

This lovely book has the power to charge your spiritual practice with new energy, and thus enable you to realize for yourself that luminosity and joy that Mitra Roshi speaks of. I am grateful that her wisdom has been made accessible to us all.

Jan Chozen Bays
Great Vow Zen Monastery

Preface

Deepening Zen: the Long Maturation, Book 2, takes the teachings offered in *Book 1* a step deeper. In teaching my students and witnessing their own ongoing, increasingly profound meditation practice, naturally the teaching needed to follow in depth. It is those later teishos (Zen talks given in the concentrated atmosphere of sesshin) that have been edited and form the material of *Book 2* as suggested by our Book Group.

What is "The Long Maturation," and why is it so important?

It started with a young Zen student who arrived at Hakuin's temple, Shōin-ji, and was admitted to his zendo for further training. This young man was only in his early twenties and he had already experienced a significant kensho. His name was Torei Enji (1721–1792). Torei had begun practice before he was nine years old and was utterly dedicated to opening fully to the profound liberation such practice can uncover.

Not long after he was training with Hakuin, he decided to do an extended solo retreat. It was winter in Japan, bitterly cold and damp, and he gave himself so fully to the urgency he felt to awaken more completely that he ignored comfort, rest and food. After many months under those conditions, he returned to Shōin-ji much deeper in his practice, but deathly ill. Doctors gave up on him, saying even if he survived the illness, which may have been TB—rampant in Japan until the dawn of antibiotics—he would not live long.

Given an imminent death sentence, Torei chose to rest, sleeping when he needed to, and otherwise writing down what he understood from his experience and knowledge of meditation practice, awakening, and the history of Zen Buddhism. He hoped it would be of help to other students. At the end of six months, he had regained his health, and decided to present his writing to Hakuin, telling him to burn it if it was not good, or to keep it and share it.

That writing has come down to us in two translations, one by the late Myokyo-ni ("Ni" designating a female priest or teacher), Rinzai Zen teacher at Shobo-an in London, England. Importantly, her translation, entitled *Discourse on the Inexhaustible Lamp*, includes the commentaries by a contemporary Rinzai master, making it more accessible to western Zen students. A more recent translation (without the commentary) by the eminent American translator, Thomas Cleary, entitled *The Undying Lamp of Zen: The Testament of Zen Master Torei*, is available through online booksellers or your local bookstore.

Torei recognized the absolute importance of not only doing zazen to come to Awakening, but to concurrently engage in what he termed, "The Long Maturation" —in other words, to bring to life in our behavior what we have opened to through our zazen. That means working to integrate the insights that naturally arise regarding our habit patterns of behavior, speech and thought. Sadly, this emphasis on expanded interior development has been lost in more recent centuries in Japanese Zen Buddhist temples and as the teaching has been brought over to the United States.

Without the inclusion of the Long Maturation, what is left of Zen practice in the U.S. was specifically dedicated to the process of coming to awakening without looking left or right, i.e., without dealing with any of the hidden issues that naturally arise as our meditation deepens. John Welwood was a longtime meditator and psychiatrist interested in spiritual awakening who saw Zen practitioners, some of whom had even become teachers, behaving in ways that belied their advanced understanding. Expressing the lack of the Long Maturation, he coined two terms to define what he felt was missing in Western meditation practices: "spiritual bypassing" and "making an end run around your issues."

In his book, *Toward a Psychology of Awakening: Buddhism, Psychotherapy and the Path of Personal and Spiritual Transformation*, Welwood defines spiritual bypassing as using "spiritual ideas and practices to sidestep personal, emotional 'unfinished business,' to shore up a shaky sense of self, or to belittle basic needs, feelings, and developmental tasks." The utter necessity of this integration of awakening into our ongoing living of life as part of zazen is emphasized in the teachings and practice at Mountain Gate.

First and foremost, Zen practice at Mountain Gate emphasizes the use of the "felt-sense" (coined by Eugene Gendlin), as well as the importance of undergoing trauma therapy, for those many people who come to spiritual practice with a history of trauma. Also, a schedule at Mountain Gate involves periods of concentrated, intensive practice alternating with sufficient time in which to process and integrate what comes to us through that intensive training. Engaging in this full range of essential practice, students of Mountain Gate have the opportunity to fully develop through both zazen and the Long Maturation, avoiding spiritual bypassing in the process. This is why we call this complete way of practicing "360-degree practice."

As with *Book 1*, *Book 2* was the creative work of our Book Group; that group of dedicated volunteers made this book possible. Daigan Leslie Ching did much of the administrative work and also compiled the list of kanji (Japanese characters) appropriate for each chapter and created the Kanji Glossary. Daishin Patrick Vigil took care of the work of obtaining permissions for quotations used in the book as well as encouraging all our efforts. Bodaiko Shannon Starkey gave essential feedback. Genshin Jeremy Cranford, a professional designer, created the perfect cover art. Hangen Justin Zeitlinger, who was a great help in editing *Book 1*, has since gone to graduate school, focusing on music composition, after his gap year at Mountain Gate. Jarad McHugh, who has a Master's degree in English Literature, was originally conceived of as Editorial Assistant. But his editing suggestions were so appropriate and outstanding that as we worked together it became clear that he was not only a co-editor but a co-author. His contributions have enriched *Book 2* enormously.

In addition to our Book Group, Yuho Thomas Kirchner verified my view of Japanese culture, especially in the context of Zen practice. Fluent in Japanese, he has lived in Japan for decades. Yuho is both a Zen monk and active Roman Catholic who has given Westerners much greater access to Buddhist texts through his excellent translations. His translation of Entangling Vines & Creepers is the only English-language version of the sole Japanese-originated collection of koans. The importance of this translation cannot be overemphasized as it makes possible the use of these unique koans in advanced Rinzai Zen practice. Jonathan Sheldon, longtime friend and fellow Zen student, gave enthusiastic reviews of the chapters sent for his comments.

Immense appreciation to Jan Chozen Bays, Roshi, longtime friend and fellow Zen practitioner, for taking time out of her incredibly busy schedule of teaching, writing and practice to read this book and write the preface.

And of course, we all, including readers of *Book 1* and future readers of *Book 2*, owe a great deal of gratitude to our publisher, John Negru, aka Karma Yönten Gyatso, head of Sumeru Press, for publishing both books. John has been a joy to work with.

Chapter One
Foundations of the Deepest Zen Practice

Torei Enji, who was the first successor of the great Zen master Hakuin, had seen remarkably deep into the true nature of reality. As you may already know, Hakuin Ekaku reinvigorated the Rinzai sect in Japan. Religions go through periods of moribundity and then they often may rise again. Someone, often one person, has a deep enough insight to bring a religion back to life. Then over the centuries that begins to fade and sinks again and somebody else hopefully brings it back to life. In the case of Rinzai Zen in Japan during the 18th century, it was Hakuin who accomplished that.

Even as a child Torei deeply yearned for understanding, for something "beyond the veil." Hakuin himself had a version of that when young. Like Torei and Hakuin, many of us open to that yearning at an early age. I remember having that sense at seven, eight, nine years old, trying to find it in the only way available to me then—which was not Buddhist. I even set up an altar under the stairway in our finished basement in Cleveland Heights and pored over the Bible that my grandmother had given me for my tenth birthday. I was searching for clues that would lead me beyond the veil. I had a sense that somehow in that book there were insights. It was too early to find them then, although now I can see gems of deep, profound wisdom in the Bible, particularly in the words of Jesus.

But Torei had the advantage of living in a country where Buddhism, which had not lost access to profound teachings, thanks to Hakuin, was available. He became a novice monk at age nine. Hakuin himself as a young boy used to go up on the hillside behind his house to do a kind of rudimentary zazen. There was also a rock there that bore some semblance to Kwan Yin, the bodhisattva of compassion. Hakuin would spend hours chanting Kwan Yin sutras, yearning to be liberated from what he was sure was a straight road to hell. He and his buddies used to play "war," lining up and throwing rocks at each other; they would also, with their slingshots, take aim at the local crows. He would also shoot his bow and arrows inside his house—certainly a forbidden activity. One day after his older brother had purchased a scroll and hung it on the *shoji*,[1] Hakuin was in the other room playing with his bow and arrows, most likely against his mother's will. One of the arrows shot through the shoji dividing the two rooms and pierced the eye of the figure on the scroll hanging on the other side.

He lived in a village on the road between Edo (nowadays called Tokyo) and the provinces, and twice a year the *daimyo*[2] were called to the presence of the shogun. Hakuin's family ran a small inn for the mid-level people accompanying those processions. The processions were a great source of entertainment, featuring jugglers, clowns, and other entertainers. Hakuin, having seen these spectacles many times growing up, eventually did paintings of them.

The temple Shōin-ji that Hakuin eventually took over is still functioning in Japan. I visited there several times and sat in that deeply powerful zendo. They also have a drum group—*taiko*, Japanese drumming—that practices there. Taiko requires deep concentration and focus, an energy that is appropriate in a zendo. A life-size, virtually alive portrait statue of Hakuin presides over the zendo from behind the altar a few steps above. Sitting on knee-high benches in a different room, practitioners at the temple chant an assortment of Kwan Yin sutras. Hakuin himself had a very deep relationship with Kwan Yin, even as a child. One day in a dream he felt a heaviness in the sleeve of his robe. Investigating, he pulled out a mirror and saw his face in it as if he were Kwan Yin. It triggered an awakening experience. Over his lifetime he painted countless images of Kwan Yin but with his own face—a deep recognition of the Oneness of all life.

Hakuin's popularity grew and many monks came to him seeking awakening. There were so many that the small temple was not able

---

1 In traditional Japanese homes, rooms are divided by "shoji", or moveable panels consisting of a wooden framework covered on both sides in Japanese paper.

2 The "daimyo" were the feudal lords of each province in Japan who were called twice a year to make a pilgrimage to Edo to meet with the shogun. This was essentially a political move intended to keep the daimyo, each who came with long processions including entertainers, from gaining too much wealth and becoming a threat to the shogun's power.

to hold all of them and they had to find their own places to live and food to eat. Some camped in the gardens and in neighboring areas. The temple was old when Hakuin moved in, having already been renovated previously by an uncle, and again had fallen into disrepair. Hakuin used to have to wear a raincoat and hat inside because the roof leaked so badly. It does rain a great deal in Japan. Torei, when he was about 20 years old, found his way to Shōin-ji and Hakuin. He'd already had a kensho and his meditation was deep.

Seriously dedicated to practice, Torei, a few years later, went on an extended solo retreat where he neglected sleep and food. It was winter in Japan, damp and cold, and he became quite ill. It's thought that the sickness may have been tuberculosis. It wasn't till many centuries later that antibiotics were discovered that could cure TB. The illness progressed until the doctors gave up on him. They said either he would die soon or his life would be otherwise short. He was in his mid-to-late twenties. We all have death sentences, but most of us assume they'll not be realized until the distant future. But for Torei that death sentence was real; he was seriously ill. So, he decided that he would simply rest and when he had enough energy, he would write down what he understood about Zen and Zen practice. With great presence, for six months, that's what he did: he rested when he felt he needed to rest, slept when he felt sleepy, and wrote about Zen practice when he had the energy to do so. During that time he slowly recovered. When Hakuin asked him to come see him, he did so and presented his writing, saying that if Hakuin deemed it worthy of sharing, to do so, but if not to burn it. Hakuin kept it.

That writing, an extensive teaching, is available today in English through Shobo-an Zen Centre, whose abbess had translated it. Myokyo-ni, ni indicating a female priest, died some years ago. Discourse on the Inexhaustible Lamp is not only a beautiful translation, but it also includes a translation of the commentary on that teaching by a 20th century Japanese roshi, Daibi.[3] It is currently available without the Daibi commentary in a translation by Thomas Cleary under the title *The Undying Lamp of Zen*.[4]

---

3   Available via Shobo-an Zen Centre's website: https://rinzaizencentre.org.uk/publications/

4   Available via most large scale book sellers including Amazon.com. https://www.amazon.com/Undying-Lamp-Zen-Testament-Master/dp/1590307925

Torei was a remarkable example of committed Zen practice. He continued to practice his entire life, dying in his early seventies despite his doctors' dire predictions. Hakuin named him a successor when he was still in his twenties, and kept trying to rope him into teaching, with minimal success. He was asked to become abbot and rebuild Ryutaku—a Rinzai temple that had fallen into disrepair—and he did do it, but he only stayed a year and then left again to go on another personal retreat. At some point he wrote the "Vow of the Bodhisattva," which we chant every morning during sesshin. The English version we chant was translated by a Spanish monk at Sōgen-ji, Dōho or Ho-san for short, and polished by Yuho Thomas Kirchner, an American monk who still lives in Japan and has worked as a translator for most of his adult life. Yuho's most important translation, Entangling Vines and Creepers, is the only Japanese collection of koans. His translation makes it possible for advanced students to work on even more koans. Torei Enji's "Bodhisattva Vow" is worth memorizing; it is a very deep teaching and a model of enlightened living:

> Disciples,
> When I humbly observe the true nature of things, all
>   are the marvelous manifestation of the Tathagata's
>   Truth. Atom by atom, instant by instant, all are
>   none other than this mysterious radiance.

Modern science has verified this. I won't get into that right now, because it's less important than the rest.

> Because of this our virtuous ancestors extended
>   loving care and reverence toward even such
>   beings as birds and beasts.
> How then, can we be but humbly grateful for the
>   food, drink and clothing that nourishes and
>   protects us throughout the day, these being in
>   essence the warm skin and flesh of the great
>   masters, the incarnate compassion of the
>   Buddha?

> If it is so even with inanimate objects, how much more should we be kind and merciful towards human beings, even those who are foolish.
> Though they become our sworn enemies, reviling and persecuting us, we should regard them as bodhisattva manifestations who in their great compassion are employing skillful means to help emancipate us from the painful karma we have produced over countless kalpas through our biased, self-centered views.
> If we awaken in ourselves this deep, pure faith, offering humble words and taking sincere refuge in our True nature, then with every thought there will bloom a lotus flower, each with a Buddha.
> These buddhas will establish Pure Lands everywhere and reveal the radiance of the Tathagata beneath our very feet.
> May we extend this mind throughout the universe, so that we and all sentient beings may equally bring to fruition the seeds of wisdom!

What about this part about being kind and merciful, even to people who are nasty to us, terrible to us, condemning us, even killing us? Let me mention something that Harada Shōdō Roshi realized personally. Harada Shōdō's father was a Buddhist priest who ran a temple in Nara along with his wife, Harada Roshi's mother. After the Meiji Restoration, things really changed for Buddhism, and a lot of Buddhist temples lost their support. Others became family temples or were owned by their supporters (or both). The priests heading those temples functioned mainly as funeral directors. Preparation comprised a two- or three-year training period in which you learn how to give a Dharma talk, how to perform certain ceremonies, how to do at least some zazen, and generally be kind of a parish priest. These people are not Zen teachers. To become a roshi—to become a Zen teacher—takes considerably longer training. In the Rinzai sect that means ongoing, intensive training for at least 20 years. And even then, you may not be ready to teach.

Harada Roshi grew up in an era when Buddhist priests were not well respected. There's a 1984 Japanese movie called *The Funeral* that expresses the Japanese disdain of Buddhist priests, many of whom since the Meiji Restoration have been relegated to conducting funeral services.[5] Young Harada had no interest in becoming a Buddhist priest. In those days, and these days as well, the male children of family priests are ordained around the age of five. So it was with him. The assumption was that he would inherit the family temple and do the same thing his father was doing. As it turned out, his older brother ended up having to become the priest there. There was an unusual case recently in Japan where there were no sons and so a daughter ended up inheriting the temple.

The young Harada wanted to become, first, an astronaut. He wanted to ride in a rocket. And then he wanted to be a pilot. Eventually, when it was time to go to college, he wanted to become a psychologist because he didn't like himself and thought that going into psychology would give him an avenue to be a better person. But one day when he was in college, his father asked him to go to school early to deliver some papers in Kyoto. He was born and raised in Nara and it's a short train ride between Nara and Kyoto where he was going to college. He was on a bus during rush hour in Kyoto when an older man dressed in priest robes got on that bus. Young Harada noticed him because he seemed unusually clear, profoundly quiet, deeply calm, and unlike any Buddhist priest he'd ever met. He was delighted to see that the man got off at the same stop that he also got off and headed to exactly the same destination Harada was to deliver the papers to. The priest was Yamada Mumon, roshi at Reiun-in, one of the four teaching sub-temple of the Rinzai headquarter temple Myoshinji. Myoshin-ji is a vast temple complex housing 43 sub-temples, most of which are no longer teaching temples, in Kyoto.

Harada was profoundly impressed by the man's demeanor. Mumon Roshi had simply, quietly made his way through the crowd, sat at the back of the bus, and began reading a little book. No fuss, no irritation about the crowd in the bus; he simply was profoundly accepting of the moment as it appeared to be. It was such a radical experience for young Harada that after he graduated, he walked

---

5   *The Funeral* IMDB https://www.imdb.com/title/tt0089746/

from Nara overland to Shōfuku-ji, in Kobe, and became a student of Yamada Mumon Roshi. Living in that teaching temple, he went to sesshin every month. But after two or three years of that schedule he still hadn't had a kensho, which disheartened him. He came out of a Rohatsu sesshin quite unhappy about it, went to Mumon Roshi and said, "I'm going into the mountains to do zazen." Mumon Roshi looked at him quietly for a minute then said to come back when he'd had kensho. So, monk Harada left and went into the mountains. By this time, he had a Buddhist name, which was Shōdō.

He camped for a year in various places in the mountains and practiced intensively. One day, a group of young people coming up the mountain to do their own quiet zazen saw him. When they saw he was dressed in robes they asked if he was a Buddhist monk. When he answered affirmatively they responded, "You are so lucky to be able to do this practice full-time! We all work and we have just one day off a week when we can come up here to meditate. How wonderful it is that you are able to do this full time!" Something in that triggered a deep awakening in Harada. He suddenly realized that all he had to do was simply receive whatever came to him. Simply receive it! That meant without ideas about whatever it was. Simply to receive the energy of the moment no matter how it appeared: frightening; challenging; embarrassing; daunting; whatever it was, simply to receive it. How? By becoming One with it where there are no opinions or judgments. That means to feel the energy of whatever reactions might be felt, by tuning in so completely that there is no felt need to react. That is the experience of the "felt sense." That's all he had to do. And he has lived by that since then. So can we.

After 20 years in the monastery, he became the fifth Dharma successor of Yamada Mumon Roshi, and was sent to Sōgen-ji, by then a quite rundown but originally very prominent temple in Okayama, Japan. He has made it his life purpose not only to bring it back to life as a deep teaching temple, but also to travel world-wide in his dedication to bring as many students as possible to awakening.

When I was training at Sōgen-ji, there were about twelve of us in residence at the beginning, and vast distances between the mats in this zendo. At every sanzen, each one of us got in to see the teacher;

it was required. The experience was quite remarkable and incredibly valuable. An intense practice—sesshin after sesshin after sesshin after sesshin after sesshin, in close proximity. Not only were there osesshin, which are "big sesshin," with fourteen hours a day of formal sitting, followed by an hour of required yaza (sitting zazen well into the night after the formal meditation for that day has ended), all of it beginning before the 4 a.m. hour of chanting, and including sanzen at least twice each day. There were only three or four days in between that osesshin and what was called kosesshin, where the schedule was almost the same except there was more work during the day and only seven hours of formal sitting. The schedule provided a big, ongoing dose of intensive practice. This was quite wondrous because you had no choice but to go deeply into your meditation, all the more so because you were in (required) sanzen twice a day during those sesshin. Each month there were three sesshin, usually one osesshin and two kosesshin.

The point in bringing up Torei Enji's "Bodhisattva Vow (Vow of the Bodhisattva)" is to share an event at Shōfuku-ji in which Harada was leading a work group—a small work party outside the inner gate of Shōfuku-ji. They were still on the Shōfuku-ji property. A group of homeless people living there felt the temple was cheating them out of water. The leader of the group, with his followers behind him, approached Harada, ready for a fight. The homeless man was described as "not a stranger to violence." Red in the face, belligerent, he stood quite close to Harada, berating him about the water. Harada, because he had had that experience of recognizing that simply receiving was all he had to do, simply received the angry man. His demeanor was one of honoring the innate perfection—the Buddha nature—of the enraged man. The person who told me this story said that he hung onto the shovel he'd been working with in case he needed to whack the guy if he took a punch at Harada. Harada was totally present and increasingly inwardly quiet. The angry man, in response, gradually quieted down, unwittingly mirroring Harada's energy. The matter was resolved and the homeless folk went away.

This remarkable resolution is described in Torei's Vow, which ends:

> If we awaken in ourselves this deep, pure faith,
> > offering humble words and taking sincere refuge
> > in our True nature, then with every thought there
> > will bloom a lotus flower, each with a Buddha.
> > These buddhas will establish Pure Lands everywhere
> > and reveal the radiance of the Tathagata beneath
> > our very feet.

What this metaphor expresses is that the awakened mind state begets awakened behavior. That is, if we've fully worked through the Long Maturation.

Many years ago, Eugene Gendlin, who has since died in his 80s, was part of a study that attempted to determine what made some people unable to transform, during even 10, 15, 20 years of psychotherapy. Others within the first three therapy sessions were changing in positive ways on the road to freeing themselves from their psychological issues. The study quickly discovered that what the three-session-transformation people were experiencing was a tuning in to what Gendlin termed the "felt sense," the sense of energy in our bodies. That tuning inward was what made the barriers dissolve, so that insight could emerge and the therapy client could move forward in their therapy.

Tuning in, allowing the felt sense to be experienced, is a vital aspect of Zen practice. When we do zazen, sit down on the cushion, extend the out-breath, experience the felt sense, the layers of seeming self-protection begin to thin. With this increasing awareness that the need to protect is an illusion, the more we open to that experience and the more capacity we have to become increasingly free of our conditioning. We become aware that we have an underlying anxiety, shame, fear, or anger, for example, that we had managed to avoid feeling through various avoidance techniques: denial, hyperactivity, addiction (not necessarily to drugs or alcohol!). Tuning into the felt sense and staying present with the energy of it, challenging as it might be, suddenly, as the Tibetan Buddhist master Longchenpa taught, the feeling is freed in its own place without having to be gotten rid of, and is transformed into pristine awareness. We have spent however long in our life trying to avoid feeling what we don't want to feel, and so we have to undo that conditioning little by little by persistent attempts to tune into that felt sense. If you tune into your body to the degree that you sort of know, for example that you're angry, but it's just a two-dimensional sense, you're still not tuning into the felt sense. If you tune in to the point where it feels three-dimensional, you suddenly are not in your head, you're not in the stories about it; you're in the felt sense. Stay with that felt sense until it dissolves! Not until it goes away, but until it dissolves. With that there's a palpable feeling of relief, like, ahh! That's a major victory toward becoming free.

To do so is essential in practice because otherwise we can bull our way through practice into a shallow kensho, and elbow aside any recognition of dysfunctional behavior that we've engaged in. That is how we have people who become Zen teachers, even Zen "masters," without being true masters, and still can abuse their students. We've seen this unfortunately in Buddhist teachers in America, and not just in America and not just in Zen. So, it's important to do this work with the felt sense in order to be able to meet challenging experiences in such a way that there "blooms a lotus flower, each with a Buddha, and these Buddhas establish Pure Lands right beneath our feet."

Everyone can do this, but there's a significant learning curve; it requires committed zazen, as well, because zazen is what will help us open to the places where we're caught and be freed from that imprisonment through our employment of the felt sense. This is vital. It's an imperative aspect of Zen practice for anyone who wants to do true Zen practice and live an authentic life.

Chapter Two
When Anxiety Comes Up in Zen Practice

A WEEK AFTER THE END of this sesshin we will begin the next sesshin—for those who attend both these sesshins it is an incredible opportunity to really double down on your practice and reap much greater benefits than you would if you went to two sesshin further apart. It's much easier than you may think.

Here I'd like to share with you something of the cultural differences impacting Zen practice in America. Japan, as a culture, has a focus on making things comfortable for people by not creating trouble for others, not creating disappointment, unhappiness, or inconvenience. An example of this is that when I was living at Sōgen-ji, one of our local supporters, a wonderful woman who had, when one of her sons died unexpectedly, chose to honor him by making monks' robes for everyone at Sōgen-ji; it was quite a gift and no doubt cost her a lot. Several years later she got stomach cancer (unrelated), which is quite common in Japan. She had surgery, and the doctors told her remaining son that her stomach cancer was gone. What they didn't tell him was that it had metastasized so she would still be dying of cancer and rather soon. It's different from how such news would be handled in the United States, where most doctors would sit down with the patient and the family and give them the difficult news, then offer plans to keep the patient comfortable, or offer additional treatment with the caveat that it would likely not extend the patient's life beyond a certain point.

Another example of the convenience for people that is so important in the Japanese culture is that you don't ordinarily ask a Japanese friend for directions to somewhere as they will feel compelled to take on the responsibility of taking you there. Then there's the transportation system: everything links. Walking the two short blocks from Sōgen-ji to the corner of the main street you can catch any number of different buses, and if it's rush hour there will usually be two or three buses on the same route clustered together, so even if the first bus is full there's going to be room on the second or third bus. As well, the buses link up to the train stations, to the airports, to the boat that can take people to the airport, and so on, and there is very little wait time between arrivals and departures. The same is true of travel in the reverse direction. Moreover, all forms of transportation leave precisely on time, down to the second. If your destination is in a remote, underpopulated area of Japan, it's not quite as prompt, but the links are all there, the more to let people come and go without inconvenience. Contrast that with my experience in the United States where I have had to wait literally hours between bus connections to get to where I needed to go. No wonder people cling to their personal vehicles.

That brings me to a different but related topic. In India nothing runs on time. You cannot count on any schedule being accurate. When Sozui—a young, newly-ordained fellow student at Sōgen-ji—and I were in India, heading to a conference of Western ordained Buddhist women in Bodh Gaya, a 24-hour train ride from Delhi, we were supposed to have been met at the airport. We weren't. We eventually got to where we were supposed to be staying and then it turned out we couldn't stay there because a whole coterie of Tibetan monks had arrived. We, being females, couldn't stay in the same place with (male) monks. So, we ended up in a guest house that we had to pay for. We had originally arranged to receive a round trip train ticket for the following morning from Delhi to Gaya. We would take a motorcycle "taxi" the few extra miles to Bodh Gaya. It turns out there was no reservation made, no available train tickets, and so we had to wait two more paying days in the guest house before there was an available space on the train. We finally were able to get a ticket on an overnight train, which was to leave the next morning at a particular time. We pointedly went to the train station two hours ahead of the departure time because you can never be sure in India of anything. We waited and waited while the train departure was still up on the board and then it vanished. At that point, we asked the person behind the thick, plastic protection screen at the counter about it and was told it would be departing from a different track at six o'clock that evening.

We returned to the guest house and then came back to the station two hours ahead of time and waited. Eventually, we found the train on a different track than scheduled and there was the ensuing crush of people trying to crash the train car. Finally, we were able elbow our way into our assigned car where we had to evict two Indian male stowaways before we could claim our bunks and settle into a night's sleep accompanied by the symphony of snores from our fellow travelers, all of them Indian men.

In the morning we realized we had no clue where to get off. There was no announcement for any of the stations we were sometimes zipping through, sometimes pausing briefly at (unlike in Japan where not only the stop is announced but which side of the train you're supposed to get off is also announced, at which point people quietly line up to exit). Moreover, the windows were so dirty, we couldn't see out. We finally had to ask one of our roommates to let us know where Gaya was. He told us it was coming up, so Sozui and I, dressed in our Buddhist robes and lugging our baggage, went out to the platform at the end of the car, ready to hop off if it simply paused. The gentleman followed us out and asked, "Are you Buddhist?" As the train slowed down, we said "yes," and he responded, "My name is Siddhartha."

We hopped off and entered the fray of motorcycle taxi drivers fighting for our presence on their motorcycles. An intense discussion ensued among the motorcycle drivers; apparently, the one who first approached us had jumped the line. We finally got on an acceptable ride and rode our way to Bodh Gaya and entered the Burmese Vihara for our conference. Of course we arrived several days late for the conference but so did everybody else because it was India. That actually turned out to be quite fortunate because the night before we arrived two foreigners were murdered in the very small town of Bodh Gaya.

Although Buddhism originated in India it had long since disappeared until Dr. B.R. Ambedkar of the Dalit (also known as Untouchable) caste himself, managed to rise to positions of prominence in post-World War II Indian government. Examining the tenets of Hinduism and Buddhism and recognizing that Hinduism supported the caste system but Buddhism did not, he converted to

Buddhism. When he did so, hundreds of thousands of Dalit people converted along with him. Hozan Alan Senauke, an American Zen Buddhist teacher and founder of the Buddhist Peace Fellowship, tapped into this movement and began going to India at least twice a year to help support and teach the Dalit Buddhists. He also helps raise funds for the group.

In addition, Hozan has been carrying out relief work in support of the Rohingya since the pogrom in Myanmar against that group of traditionally Muslim Burmese.[1] Whether or not the Rohingya are Muslims doesn't matter to an authentic Buddhist; these are people in pain. Buddhist practice is concerned with relieving (and not causing) suffering. Hozan goes where there is suffering, working to relieve it.

I give you this background because I want to bring up something else which is very, very common in Zen practice. To illustrate this, I'd like to share with you a piece from a book he's just written: Alan is riding in a cab from the Kolkata (Calcutta) airport to his hotel. Alan and the taxi driver have no shared language and it becomes clear that the driver can't find the hotel. After a good deal of zigzagging about in the darkness the driver stops his cab in the middle of a street and wordlessly ushers Alan out, puts his baggage into a nearby rickshaw, and drives away. Alan climbs into the rickshaw and the rickshaw peddler pulls him through the Kolkata night to his hotel. No words were spoken in this episode but the teaching seems to be that when you're anxious because of being in an unfamiliar situation, then if you see that you're not in evident danger, you have the chance to go into not knowing. It's a credit to Hozan's own Zen practice that he had reached a place where that experience would not have made him anxious.

As we get deeper in our practice, we can reach a place of sensing danger. This is actually the "edge of the cliff." "Let go your hold on the edge of the cliff and leap, hands held high, into the fiery abyss" is a common refrain in Zen. We are so invested in a sense of self—a self-image—that it can be frightening to feel we are losing a grip on it. And that grip must necessarily be let go if we are to open into

---

[1] The pogrom against the Muslim Rohingya in Myanmar has been encouraged by a "Buddhist" priest. There is very little real training for Buddhist monks in Myanmar these days. Moreover, it is for many a cushy way of life in Myanmar. A true Buddhist would never behave in such ways as to encourage suffering.

the profound understanding of who and what we really are: the true nature of reality. (Some people don't even recognize that fear is stopping them because they hold themselves back from it so intensely.) Clearly, Alan had crossed that threshold and so was unafraid and open to the unknown when his taxi driver stopped in the middle of a street and put Alan's baggage into the rickshaw. The cabbie no doubt uttered some words incomprehensible to Alan as he gave the address to the rickshaw driver. To be sure, Alan would have had a sense of the okayness of the situation, so had not simply been stupid. When one has let go of enough of one's conditioning (what created the self-image) and done enough of the long maturation, one also is more able to sense situations clearly and understand whether there is real danger or not.

When our zazen has gone deep enough to bring us to the edge of that "cliff" there's almost a sobering "smell" of intense danger but it can be too much at that point in some people's practice. Persist in the practice and continue tasting the danger and one day you'll be able to leap off the edge of that cliff into a level of true freedom. We can become free in ways we cannot even fathom, but there are levels of that freedom depending on how completely we are letting go of that self-image and that conditioning, at least temporarily. What necessarily must follow is the long maturation if the experience of that freedom is to be continued and deepened. This process can be likened to a tidal wave—the water, or self-image, goes out to reveal the Truth that was hidden, the wave of conditioning then returns, though in this case weakened. This makes it imperative that the work of the long maturation is taken up to further weaken and eventually release that now seen through, to whatever degree, self-image.

To reach the depth of that freedom it's important to walk into and allow yourself to experience fully the smell of that cliff, that insecurity, that not knowing, even as frightening or terrifying as it will seem to be. This is why a commitment to practice is so vital; without persisting in it and without the faith that we can actually get to the other side of the dismal swamp that we may be struggling through we won't get there. It's called practice because for a long time it does require practice. Eventually it becomes a natural way of living.

When I was at the Rochester Zen Center long ago, I noticed that while about 50 or 60 people would come to the day-long Zen workshops that were offered, maybe 10 of them would start coming to sittings. The number would fall off over the months to maybe two or three who stuck it out long term. Back in Roshi Kapleau's heyday, every Sunday morning roughly 300 people would come for the sitting and teisho; they'd be sitting three-deep in the Buddha Hall and in every possible place to sit in the main building—hallways, dokusan waiting line, basement sitting room, etc. But as the weeks went by, I began to realize that within the 300-plus people there were only about 30 regulars, people who really persisted. People have to want to do the practice, be committed to do the practice, and be willing to do the practice long term to reap the fruits promised of practice. That means being willing to use the felt-sense to walk into every difficult inner and outer experience that comes before us.

We are conditioned even in the womb before birth and subsequently as well, and the conditioning creates a self-image. We open to our environment and that environment reacts or responds to us; someone smiles at us, or when we're wet and hungry nobody comes despite our cries. We conclude things about ourselves as a result of those experiences—I'm unlikeable, I'm no good, I can trust people, I can't trust people—and our behavior reflects these assumptions. Thus, we adopt a self-image and live through the lens of that self-image. Yet, in reality, we are worthy of respect, worthy of love and compassion, worthy of honor. Because of that conditioning we behave in ways that contradict our inherent self-worth. (It is the person that is worthy, not necessarily the behavior.)

For people who persist long enough, even those who have been traumatized, if we do our Zen practice deeply enough for long enough, we will awaken to that amazingness that truly is. But along the way there's a lot of conditioning. It's critical to open to that conditioning in order to relieve its grip. Yet we have an investment in not opening to it. This doesn't necessarily mean that if we've been traumatized we need to remember in detail the trauma. We don't always have an explicit memory of a situation, nor do we need to. Our body knows and it's locked in our body, and not necessarily accessible through words. But the sensations of danger and terror remain stored within us and are readily triggered.

With the guidance of an appropriately trained trauma therapist in concert with the use of the felt-sense in our zazen, conditioning can be gradually released, opening us to the experience of being caught less and less by that history. Without that combination of vital work, we will be easily triggered and react in ways that are not in alignment with our inherent self-worth. Sounds daunting, but it does get easier. The combination of Zen practice and appropriate therapy is far more potent than either of them alone. With the combination of the two processes we will find ourselves less invested in a need to tightly control our environment and limit our openness to experience.

Right out of college, my husband was accepted as a new Foreign Service Officer (International diplomat under the United States State Department). As a new Foreign Service Officer he received several months of important training, both technical and cultural. One of the areas they were concerned with was the impact of foreign cultures on a person's psychological health, especially those cultures that were very different (i.e., unfamiliar) from Western culture. My husband was fortunate enough to receive eight months of full-time training in the Burmese language, the writing system of which is completely different from Roman characters. I was also able to learn to speak and read a certain amount of Burmese, but most of the other foreign service families who were assigned to Yangon (Rangoon) did not receive the language training.

During the rainy season in Yangon it rained 24/7 for months. The gloom brought many foreigners to a deep depression. The soil became so water-logged that huge trees would topple. Even your underwear had to be ironed in order to dry enough to comfortably wear it. The buildings were moldy. Even the fur on the cows was moldy! There was trash everywhere and a sense of faded elegance in the city. Yet it was an amazing experience to live in that country—the golden pagodas, the Burmese women squatting with their basket of wares, smoking their big fat cheroots, the sidewalks covered with splats of betelnut juice, the experience of never getting dry in the rainy season, and in the rest of the year the hot steaminess of the atmosphere, always the potential for amoebic and other types of dysentery, and a strange, unintelligible language to people who had no study of it. You couldn't even read the street signs. These factors made it very challenging for many Embassy employees and their families to live in that environment. There are parallels to this kind of experience in Zen practice. It's impossible to give specific instructions as to how to come to awakening. For a long time we have no clue if we're making progress or not. This can be unsettling to people who have gone through an entire education system of being graded and having constant feedback on their progress. Moreover, in Zen practice, we're opening to our fears and conditioning. The work of Zen cannot be done with words, yet we are so trained to use words to solve problems.

The foreigners' anxiety was palpable. This was true of the Europeans as well. People reacted in many different ways to the stress of this strange environment. One American wife committed suicide by jumping out a hospital's third story window. A European diplomat hung himself in his closet three days before he was due to return to his country. Another American wife, so terrified of her children getting ill, insisted that her servants, three times a day, boil water, haul it upstairs, and bathe the three children. People normally not extreme, turned to alcohol, illicit relationships, and other means to deal with the anxiety.

For a person who's been traumatized, many of the same means of dealing with that suffering are adopted. If we've had any untoward experiences growing up that makes it imperative for us to really feel in control of our environment. Now, Zen practice will begin to erode that control necessarily because in order to come to awakening you have to let go of everything, especially control. It is a very frightening proposition for many people; it certainly was for me. I remember being terrified of going into dokusan, certain that Roshi could see right through me, which I'm sure he could. It was during that period in my practice that I had a repetitive nightmare in which I would find myself in the middle of a vast ballroom, filled with maybe 500 people, and suddenly realized I didn't have a stitch of clothes on while everyone else was dressed. Anxiously looking for a way to escape, I realized that if I tried to streak through the crowd toward any of the exits, all of which were far away, it would be more noticeable than if I just stood there naked. Soon after, another repetitive nightmare expressed my sense of losing control. I was driving into a parking lot, pulling into a parking space, and suddenly the brakes didn't work – I couldn't stop. I'd anxiously throw the car into reverse and speed backwards still out of control. Needless to say, it was a very challenging period in my Zen practice. I went through a lot of my earlier sesshin shut down (dissociated) because, due to my history of trauma, it was too frightening to be present. But having recognized years before that there was no alternative to a life of suffering except going inward, I persisted in my concentrated zazen.

To be present, attentive, and aware is an essential prerequisite to coming to awakening. While I was mostly dissociated for some of the early years in my Zen practice, that practice bolstered by the recognition that it was the only way to freedom, eventually brought me to a place where little by little I was able to be present, particularly allowing myself to feel the energy of the sense of danger and the terror that had always been beneath the radar. I also in different periods of my life underwent psychotherapy. Through this daunting work, eventually I emerged from that life experience filled with terrifying dangers into the sunshine and a level of ease and freedom I had seemingly never known before. I say "seemingly" because since I had been a child, I'd sensed there was something barely out of reach that was more clear, different, and free than what I was experiencing.

Chapter Three
The Challenge of Letting Go

I'D LIKE TO SHARE some of the words of an ancient Chinese *Chan* master, Huang Po, who was also known as Obaku—the Japanese pronunciation of his Chinese characters. He was the teacher of Rinzai. *A Bird in Flight Leaves No Trace* is a collection of Huang Po's writings, originally translated by John Blofeld, newly translated under that title by Robert Buswell with commentary by Seon Master Subul.[1]

The title, *A Bird in Flight Leaves No Trace*, refers to the mind of utter awareness of one who has completely let go of any smell of self-image. We all are endowed with that mind, but for most people it's submerged under the effects of our conditioning. Initially, with enough zazen, we may open briefly to it, but then the long maturation is necessary to completely reveal it. When we live from that let go mind there's no outside or inside. There's no sense of a "me." It's impossible to express this truth in language; this is why we have to go beyond words when we are doing our Zen practice. It is where we will experience our face before our parents were born. When we have let go to that degree, we leave no traces. There's no residual energy trailing after us. I think here of when I met Mario Montese, a Swiss Italian man who became a rockstar when he was 19 years old and was asked to join Heatwave, a soul-funk band of the '70s. Mario said the group members had some heavy karma—five members of the band died violently or died through drug use.

After many years of playing with the band, one very early morning, Mario was coming out of a publicity party and heading

---

[1] Robert Buswell who spent years as a monk in a major Buddhist monastery in Korea and eventually became Distinguished Professor of Buddhist Studies at UCLA is an excellent translator of Asian Buddhist texts. If you'd like to know about his time as a monk, read *The Zen Monastic Experience* by Robert Buswell Jr., Princeton University Press, 1993. Master Subul Sunim is a highly regarded master of the Korean "Meditation" school. He presides over the Anguk Seonwon in Busan, a large center of Buddhist practice in Korea.

home to his wife and one-year-old son when he was stabbed in the heart by an unknown assailant. He woke up after six weeks in a hospital, unable to speak, see, or move; he was completely paralyzed. The only thing he could do was hear. Doctors told Mario he had been clinically dead for 6-8 minutes before he was found and resuscitated.[2]

When he was in the hospital after that attack, he focused on the big toe of one foot; after three months, he was able to move the toe, after five months, he was able to see light and dark, and after a year he was able to see clearly. Gradually, his other abilities, such as walking, began to return. Thought would have inhibited this healing process. He was not able to think for many months and said that when he could think again it was a great disappointment; suddenly, there was a subtle separation from the experience of reality. To be sure, he has continued to have some evidence of remaining neurological damage. The intense presence that was required in his healing, and the challenge of having lost everything,[3] brought him to a place of deep spiritual awareness and presence where he left no traces. When I closed my eyes in his presence, there was no sense of anybody else being there.

Let me share with you some of the words of Huang Po. I'll also share some of the comments of Seon Master Subul, whose first American temple was recently opened in Los Angeles. Here are Huang Po's words, "All the buddhas and sentient beings are only the one mind; there is no other dharma.[4] Since time immemorial, this mind has never been produced or extinguished." Our true reality has neither been produced nor extinguished, it neither exists nor

---

[2] Death is not as instantaneous as we generally assume even if it appears sudden. Interestingly, as our dying process unfolds, it is said that hearing is the last sense to dissolve. Depending on how tightly attached a person is to this life, it can take some time before the death process completes. This is why in Buddhism when someone dies we don't do anything to disrupt the body such as cremation or embalming for at least five days as it would interrupt the death process and delay its completion. When doing funeral services, chanting is directed toward the deceased and the deceased is spoken to in a final attempt to awaken the person to the Truth.

[3] His wife left him as did his much loved music career and, initially, his ability to move, see, and communicate. Although, by sixteen years later, when I met him, he had developed a close relationship with his son and had a long-term relationship with a wonderful girlfriend with whom he still lives.

[4] When dharma is written with a small-d, it refers to phenomenon, meaning "thing," but in this case "thing" does not apply. Something like "suchness" would be more appropriate. When it is written with a capital-D, it refers to the teaching of the Buddha.

doesn't exist. Yes, people are born, yes, people die, and the mind is not separate from that.

And that can bring forth some puzzlement.[5] And that is excellent because it is through puzzlement and the necessary going beyond words that we can awaken to that profound truth that Huang Po is speaking of. "This mind has never been produced or extinguished. It is neither green nor yellow; it has neither form or characteristics. It does not belong to the categories of either existence or non-existence. It cannot be measured in terms of new or old, long or short, large or small. It transcends all limits, measures, names, traces, and comparisons. What is right in front of you—that is it. But if you start to think, you will be far off the mark." Which means we have to search not through thought (i.e., words) because thought cannot reach that which we seek to open to. There's a saying in Korean Seon, turn the light inward and trace the radiance down to its source. And that is exactly what we are working to do in our Zen practice.

We normally focus outside of ourselves, engage with things, and with people, and in actions, and thinking about them, but we need time to focus inside as well. It is through focusing inside and opening to we don't even know what, but tracing down the radiance to its source. This in a nutshell is our Zen practice and this is what will bring about awakening. Regardless of our religion, spiritual practices such as prayer and meditation, or even if we have none, interior focusing beyond words is the only way to awaken to that Truth.[6] Flora Courtois is an example of this interior focusing driven by that puzzlement.[7] In Rinzai Zen, we have our expedient means to help us focus; for example, the extended-out breath. Another example is

---

5   One of the three pillars or prerequisites for effective zazen that will bring us to awakening is "doubt," or "perplexity." The other two are "determination" to persist however long it takes and "faith" that we can eventually awaken to the truth.

6   For readers of a Christian leaning, *The Cloud of Unknowing: And The Book of Privy Counseling* by author unknown, 1994, is an excellent guide.

7   Flora Courtois (1916–2000) was an American woman who had an experience of enlightenment as a college student after much interior searching. You can read her inspiring story in a later chapter of *The Hazy Moon of Enlightenment* by Taizan Maezumi Roshi and Bernie Glassman. Be sure to get the latest edition of this book because earlier versions of the book do not have her story. When Flora died she left the rights to her story to Zen Center of Los Angeles where she had eventually trained extensively in Zen. They chose to publish it as an additional two chapters in *The Hazy Moon of Enlightenment*.

the use of a *koan* to help us explore that sense of something missing (perplexity), which is a universal experience and naturally comes up for people. A traditional koan can help us to focus the perplexity but the koan is not essential. What is essential is the perplexity. We're all seeking for that ineffable Reality.

Working with that sense of something missing, with openness to possibility, can bring us to profound presence and Reality. Here's what Master Subul writes about this, "people can handle what they can understand, but when they come across something incomprehensible, they become puzzled and feel pushed to the edge of a precipice. At that moment they become eager to secure rational understanding without being aware that they're doing so. However, when you let all things go, you no longer care whether a certain thought arises or not. This is because nothing affects a practitioner who experiences no thought." And no thought is not blankness; no thought is a state of such presence that there aren't any thoughts demanding attention in your mind. There is awareness. You understand intimately where you are in each moment, but there's nothing driving any need to perform, any need to be somebody, any need to do anything but be fully present and respond to whatever circumstances might need a response.

When we experience that total presence, the normal "yada-yada," the background noise in our mind, the need to plan and think is gone, at least temporarily. Instead, from that state of mind can arise, without hindrance, a clear direction to move in. When we have experienced deeply enough that state of profound presence, we are later able, even in the midst of the work of the long maturation, to drop into it at will. When we do drop in, whatever direction we need to move in is naturally, wordlessly revealed. There's a sense within us that says, but not with words, go this direction. And when we move in that direction, in my experience at least, it works 100 percent of the time. It may not be what we expect, it may not be the direction we assume we ought to go in, or want to go in, but if we go with it, it is always right. An essential prerequisite of this freed up mind state is sufficient letting go of investment in a self-image. I have a couple of examples in my own life as some of you may have already heard. It needs to be said, however, that we must work with our fear of letting go and take the risk to jump off that precipice, otherwise we won't experience the profound presence of that essential letting go of our self-image.

It was an experience of meeting the precipice while I was living in Turkey after my life crashed and I lost everything that mattered to me and I had no other choice but to begin Zen practice. Eventually, it became clear that in order to be pushed to practice I would need to do residential training at the Rochester Zen Center as I was unable to practice with any regularity on my own. At the time, I had very little income and could barely afford a plane ticket to Rochester. There was not enough money to bring my belongings, including my beloved antique brass bed that had belonged to my grandparents, back to the United States with me. I had no idea whether I could get a job in Rochester, or whether I'd be accepted to live and train at the Rochester Zen Center, but there was such a strong sense that it was the right move regardless of these unknowns and what I would have to leave behind. Against all logic, I took the risk and went. Although it took eight months before I was accepted to residential training at the Rochester Zen Center, and in the meantime cleaned houses for a living, it was exactly the right thing to do. I have never had any regrets.

The more recent example was when I chose with a clear, strong sense of the rightness of the move, to locate Mountain Gate up in this remote Northern New Mexico valley far away from large cities or any city for that matter. We're in the middle of a tiny, little unincorporated village, which boasts something like 140 families spread down the three roads that comprise the village. It might have made more sense, or it seemed to make more sense, to simply locate in Santa Fe where people were. As a result of this, and the choice, initially, to not establish a website, Mountain Gate was totally anonymous. Historically, the temples of the masters of old in China were hidden away in the mountains. This is also true in Taiwan today. Locating these temples remotely naturally produces barriers. Despite its remote location, people who have needed to find Mountain Gate have found it, and so the practice is deep and strong here.

In Japan, traditionally, to enter a Zen monastery, there are multiple barriers one must pass through before admission to practice in the temple. If you're living locally in Japan, you actually have to do something called "waiting in the garden." You go to a Zen training monastery with a letter from your ordaining priest and a letter from you, strongly pledging your ongoing and intense commitment to do Zen training at that temple. You put your head down on the step of the common work entrance (as opposed to the entrance where people arrive for ceremonies and other public occasions) and ask for admission. A monk will usually come out and say, "sorry, we don't have any room here." Or, they might say, "you don't look like you've got what it takes to train here, go away." They may come out if you persist, which you better do if you really want to train there, and whack you with the *keisaku* multiple times. They may pick you up and bodily throw you out, but if you persist for four, five, six, seven days, head down on the step, then they may bring you into a room, close to the entrance, that only has two walls and perhaps a sitting cushion. It's in a rather central area so anybody moving by will see what you're doing. If you sit there and do committed zazen 24 hours a day, after a few days, they'll say, "you can train here for now, but you can't sit in the zendo. You'll have to sit on the *gai tan*." (They will probably, surreptitiously bring you some food here and there during your long trial period in the two-walled room and perhaps while your head is down on the *genkan* step).

For westerners going to Sōgen-ji, although you likely won't have to wait in the garden, there are multiple barriers as well before one is accepted to the temple. Harada Shōdō Roshi requires that the first barrier is to attend a sesshin in your own country with him. There are further barriers, including the cost of buying a plane ticket to Japan and traveling to Sōgen-ji without knowing the language. There is culture shock that can hit months after arrival, especially as the honeymoon period ends and the reality of not knowing the language and the intensity of the training sets in. If you're fluent in Japanese already, that's a major advantage. Then there is the rigorous schedule; you'll likely only get at most four to five hours or less of sleep within each 24 hours. Even after that there is the further challenge of the months of extreme cold without the possibility of getting warm, months of extreme heat and humidity with no air conditioning, and the clouds of mosquitoes. If you open to these challenges, they can impel you to greater presence and significantly deeper practice, including potentially jumping off that metaphorical cliff and coming to some level of awakening.[8] No one is allowed to leave during an official training period and the training periods at Sōgen-ji run from February to August and August to February with no breaks in between. Most foreigners have no way of comprehending the extremity of these challenges before arriving in Japan. Going as a tourist, there's no similarity. The environment of a Zen temple is very different from a tourist experience where you can go clothed as you wish, and where there's air conditioned and heated hotels, buses, trains, department stores, etc.

When young Harada, who wanted nothing to do with becoming a temple priest, saw Yamada Mumon Roshi getting on the bus, quietly making his way to the back, sitting down and reading a small book, all while leaving no trace, it completely changed the course of Harada's life. The experience of witnessing a person so let go, so impressed the young man that instead of becoming a psychologist after college, he walked over the hills from Kyoto to Kobe and became a student and eventual successor of Yamada Mumon Roshi at Shōfuku-ji.

When I finished my formal training at Rochester, I still felt the need to further deepen my understanding, rather than go out and start a temple or Zen Center of my own. I had already met and connected with Harada-roshi at Rochester Zen Center. Shortly after that, someone had gifted me a sesshin with Harada-roshi in the Pacific Northwest. I took three months off from Rochester, went to Japan, spent two months at Sōgen-ji, a couple weeks in Kyoto sitting with Morinaga Soko Roshi's group, following that I attended a Rohatsu sesshin with Harada Tangen Roshi at Bukkoku-ji in Obama. I then went back to the United States firm in my deep sense that I needed to return to Sōgen-ji for ongoing training.

On my return to the States, I came down with hepatitis while teaching in Mexico. I had barely recovered when I then got meningitis, which morphed into encephalitis, and finally a secondary

---

8   To paraphrase a koan: a monk asked the master, "how can I deal with heat and cold?" The master responds, "Go where there is no heat or cold." To which the monk says, "Where's that?" The master answers, "When hot, die to the heat; when cold, die to the cold." This is not urging the monk to tune out, but rather to tune in to the physical experience so fully that there is only the physical experience and not the judgemental mind commenting on it.

infection that paralyzed half my face. Many people told me it was stupid to go back to Japan, but again that firm, deep, sense that it was the right thing to do was there and I followed it. I returned to Japan for intensive training at Sōgen-ji. When you're open to that deep, clear, inner sense, and move on it, when the self-image is not driving your perception, you leave no trace. But, if instead, you only cogitate about it, there are plenty of traces flowing behind you. To leave no trace, you have to be let go to the point of being able to be completely one with each moment.

This is the kind of thing that you can open to if you allow yourself to stay truly present without having a fixed agenda. That doesn't mean that you don't have plans. I did have to get enough money together to make the journey, but how to do that also came with a deep sense of what to do. So it continued and I went to Japan. It's not about floating along in the sky somewhere in some ethereal mind state. It's about being so totally present that there's nobody being present and therefore the right direction naturally becomes known and you can move in that direction. Again, in my experience, because I've experienced this kind of thing multiple times in my life, each time it has turned out to be exactly the right thing to do, but in order to reach that point we have to do sufficient zazen, which entails letting go of the self-image that has to be somebody. That can also require working through any difficult history we've had because we can't just jump from one mind state to complete openness. There's a process that has to be undergone and that process is undergone through our Zen practice.

When we reach a point where we can't hang on to intellectual understanding, we reach a precipice and then comes the classic admonition "let go your hold on the cliff and leap hands held high into the fiery abyss." It can actually feel like standing on the edge of a cliff and having no choice but to leap to your death. Ultimately, to come to awakening you'll need to do that for leaping off the precipice is a metaphor for letting go of an investment in your self-identity. It's rarely a permanent letting go at first, because rarely do people completely let go with the first jump. It is usually, however, enough of a letting go that the benefits of letting go become obvious: insight into what Huang Po is expressing, the freedom to live more completely, without the misperceptions engendered by a self-image.

Just as if we were faced with an actual cliff that we were ordered to jump off to our death, a great deal of fear can come up as we get close to that metaphorical precipice. Courage and persistence are required to reach that edge and jump. It's not necessarily a permanent letting go by any means; we come back into our old life, but we now see it with new eyes and we realize that certain things that we held dear really are irrelevant now. It becomes easier to let go of things, but we are still faced with our karmic baggage and that is essential to work through if we are to be totally free. It's a grave misunderstanding that having a kensho experience is your home free. You have an opening and you can choose to continue moving in that direction and open further and deeper, or you can sit on your laurels and play with it like a fancy toy, in which case it will eventually fade. But persist and you'll be more and more able to live freely without leaving a trace and know for yourself what Huang Po is speaking of.

Chapter Four
Escape is Not a Solution

Chapter One
Escape Is Not a Solution

Although there are times in our life when escape is an appropriate response, when it comes to our Zen practice, it can be of great benefit not to try to escape. This is why the schedule and the rules in a Zen temple or monastery are limiting and can seem to be constraining. It is not acceptable, for example, to move during the sitting period. That limits us from trying to escape an uncomfortable mind state by distracting ourselves by moving. There's a fixed schedule, and we're expected to go by it, which can limit our personal activities. These rules are important tools in our training for if our opportunities to escape are limited, we're forced to confront and face the discomfort that may have come up as a result of our attachments to the seeming freedom of being able to do whatever we want to do whenever we want to do it.

In the previous chapter, Korean Seon Master Subul Sunim was quoted as follows, "People can handle what they can understand, but when they come across something incomprehensible, they become puzzled and feel pushed to the edge of a precipice. At that moment they become eager to secure rational understanding without being aware that they're doing so." It is not escaping, but rather going right into the confusion, frustration, anger, sadness, restlessness, whatever the mind state is, and wordlessly exploring it that offers the potential to become free of it. To awaken to the truth that we are not this accumulated conditioning that skews our vision and causes us to react rather than respond to circumstances is known as satori. The reality is that that conditioning, while certainly real in the relative sense, results in a persona that is not our real self. Driven by that we live and interact in ways that perpetuate the discomfort that causes us suffering interspersed with fleeting moments of happiness.

The freedom that comes through awakening is unlike what we usually think of as freedom. It is an extraordinary freedom that goes far beyond doing whatever we want because we want to do it. We're free to not be hooked by uncomfortable circumstances. We're free to fully accept them and do what is appropriate in response. If there's appropriate action to be taken, we are able to move freely to take it. But if, like Jacque Lusseyran,[1] after he experienced his awakening, we're caught in an inescapable circumstance, we're able to receive it without the normal anguish that might otherwise be there because we're attached to what we don't want to be there. Here the operant word is "attached."

I'd like to share with you a koan—case 16 from the *Mumonkan* collection—that illustrates the freedom that one can experience of letting go the attachment to being somebody with a particular identity with ideas about what we want and don't want that come with that attachment. Yun-men said, "The world is vast and wide. Why do you put on your seven-piece robe at the sound of the bell?" In other words, why, if you're so awakened and therefore so free, do you put on your *kesa* and go into the *hondo* to do the morning chanting on schedule, fulfilling that responsibility as a temple priest, instead of heading out for coffee with a friend? When we are able to let go to that degree, life flows. We're deeply okay with going into the hondo at four a.m. even if we've been up late the night before.

Though most of us are not temple priests, all of us have responsibilities in our lives. Even if we're children we have a responsibility to go to school on time and not play hooky; if we are adults with a job, we have a responsibility to go to the job at the proper time and fulfill the work of that job to the best of our abilities; if we're a new parent with a baby that has to be fed every three to four hours, but we're exhausted from not enough sleep, we still get up to take care of the baby. If we have not let go sufficiently our ideas about ourselves, we're unable to do those things without a great deal of interior friction and resistance. This is the difference between having a degree of awakening with a commitment to continuing work on the long maturation or not. The awakened one simply moves and serves the moment without any need to complain or be upset. While for one not yet awakened, we may not like it, we may get

---

[1] Jacques Lusseyran was imprisoned in the death camp, Buchenwald, during the second World War. You can read his full story in his autobiography, *And There Was Light: The Extraordinary Memoir of a Blind Hero of the French Resistance in World War II*.

angry about it, or at least irritated, and in extreme cases we may just abandon the duty.

In order to reach that free mind state expressed in that koan, we need to let go of what is preventing us from experiencing it. That is a frightening thing to do. So frightening, it's not so different from standing on the edge of a cliff a thousand feet high and being forced to jump off. What is that precipice? In the second Noble Truth, the Buddha said that our discomfort, or if you want to call it suffering, comes as a result of clinging to what we want: we want to escape unpleasant circumstances, we're frustrated when things don't come out the way we want them to, we're unhappy when someone we care about leaves, and we don't like it when someone we don't like is in our presence or ordering us around. But the most intense clinging is to the subtle sense we have of who we assume we are. That image, of course, is created through our life experience and our ideas about them; in other words, our conditioning. If we try to escape in our Zen practice, we lose an incredible opportunity. But within the context of Zen practice and sometimes within the context of life itself, when we find ourselves in the mind state that Subul Sunim is referring to, trying to escape an uncomfortable, perhaps even painful mindset, eliminates a potential opportunity to come to awakening. The precipice represents the point at which we must let go of that self-image or stay stuck in the *dukkha* of an endless round of challenging mind states.

Coming to awakening and engaging in the ongoing exploration and letting go that is made possible through the work of the long maturation takes time. But as long as we continue, we are being transformed whether we realize it or not. With this work, the walls of our self-imprisonment begin to melt away. There are several koans starring Tung-shan Liang-chieh (also known as Tokusan, Deshan Xuanjian, Te-shan Hsuan-chien, and Senkan) that together illustrate the progress of this transformation. In case number 4 in the *Hekiganroku*, also known as the *Blue Cliff Record* or the *Blue Rock Record*, Tokusan starts off as a feisty monk, newly awakened and full of Zen sickness.[2] Because he was not yet grounded in the reality

---

2 Zen sickness commonly describes a person who has newly experienced a kensho and has not yet become grounded within this new openness and understanding.

revealed through his recent awakening, and full of his newfound freedom, he did some inappropriate things.

He was free up to a point and so he engaged in that freedom without any sensibility. The first case reads as follows, when Tokusan arrived at Kuei Shan,[3] he walked straight into the teaching hall without taking off his sandals or leaving his traveler's bundle outside the door, ignoring protocol. He crossed from east to west and from west to east and said, "There's nothing, no one," and walked out. When he got to the monastery gate, he said to himself, "Still, I shouldn't be so coarse," and returned to the teaching hall, this time removing his sandals and putting down his bundle. "He reentered the hall with full ceremony to meet Kuei Shan. As Kuei Shan sat there, Tokusan held up his sitting mat and said, 'Teacher!' Kuei Shan reached for his whisk, whereupon Tokusan shouted, shook out his sleeves and left."

In case 13 of the *Mumonkan*, Tokusan occurs again, this time decades later as an elder teacher, humble, and free of a self-image. The koan reads, Tokusan went to the dining room carrying his bowls. Seppō, *tenzo*[4] at the time, said to him, "Old teacher, where are you going? The meal gong has not been struck yet." Humbly and without a word, Tokusan simply returned to his room and waited for the gong. Please note that not only had Tokusan long ago had a deep realization and no doubt had further insights subsequently and had also done decades of the work of the long maturation. By this time he was not only free—truly free—but also seasoned and grounded in that freedom. Thus he was simply not irritated or annoyed or embarrassed when Seppō told him it wasn't meal time yet. Compare Tokusan's behavior at this point in his older years as a seasoned teacher with that first koan in which he brashly walks into the teaching hall with his shoes on, which is quite inappropriate.

It takes a long time of dedicated, committed practice to progress between our version of Tokusan as a newly awakened monk to an increasingly free and mature life, whether or not we become a Zen teacher. But it's not all grueling. In the early years, when we're more caught in the products of our conditioning, the practice is much

---

3   In ancient times in China, the masters were usually known by the name of the mountain on which they established their monastery.

4   The head cook in the monastery. Normally a position held by an experienced monk.

more difficult than it is as time goes on and we gradually become freer. The work of the long maturation becomes joyful as that time goes by. Joyful because we are gradually letting go of where we are attached and therefore experiencing increasing freedom from our habit patterns.

Tokusan (Deshan) as well as other now famous Chan masters such as Jōshu lived during a tumultuous time in Tang Dynasty China—a time not so different from what we are experiencing here in the world these days. No doubt the chaos, violence, political upheaval, and the personal need to make sense of all of it and find a place of internal safety inspired the continuing deepening of their practice. The An Lushan Rebellion (755–763) shook everything up and began a decline of central authority, which led to violence and mayhem. It was during this period that those remarkable Buddhist teachers lived and taught.

And that's something to keep in mind because when things get rough and we can't count on anything such as safety, food, or support, then we're forced to find other resources for seeming stability. This is part of the point of another koan. In case 43 of the *Hekiganroku*, "A monk said to Tōzan, 'Cold and heat descend upon us. How can we avoid them?' Tōzan said, 'Why don't you go where there is no cold or heat?'" The monk asked where is that, and Tōzan replied, "When cold, die to the cold. When hot, die to the heat."

What does that really mean? Let's give an example of how this can be experienced by someone who has been deeply awakened. Ganto came to awakening quite a bit sooner than his buddy Seppō, and was teaching in his own temple by the time he was in his early 50s. It was during that time of political unrest in China when violence and robberies were frequent that Ganto's temple was overrun by bandits. For whatever reason, they killed Ganto by skewering him with a sword. As he was being killed, he screamed so loud that it was heard three leagues (nine miles) away.

This scream for some with not yet understanding could be interpreted as a descent into hell as Ganto died. Hakuin had become a Buddhist monk at the age of 14 convinced that was the only way to escape a sure road to hell for his boyish escapades and now he's hearing about Ganto, a Buddhist monk, screaming as he's being murdered. In an effort to understand the fear Hakuin must have felt, you can visit in more recent times in Singapore, Hong Kong, and Yangon, what are known as Tiger Balm Gardens. "Tiger Balm" because the creator of Tiger Balm, which is used extensively as a healing ointment in Asia and the West, was quite wealthy. He was a devout Buddhist and established these gardens, which were full of the depictions of Buddhist hells to inspire other Buddhists to stay the path. You can, for example in the Singapore garden, walk through one of the ice hells. There are other hells depicting people being run through with swords, boiled in oil, or otherwise tortured. Although hell is really within one's own mind and imagination, these images, long before the Tiger Balm gardens, were made known to the ten-year-old Hakuin to the point of terrifying him.

He had begun his practice initially in a non-Zen, non-meditation Buddhist sect. Although a few years later he did start Zen practice. Having become a Buddhist monk in order to escape the suffering of hell, when he heard the story of what Ganto did as he was dying, Hakuin was so disheartened that for some months he left Zen practice, apprenticing himself to a master calligrapher. However, when he realized that he would most likely not make it as a calligrapher, unsure of the direction he should take, he entered a Zen temple courtyard during a time when the temple scrolls were being aired out to prevent them from getting moldy in the overwhelming dampness of Japan. Seeking guidance, he was moved to close his eyes, put his finger down on one of those scrolls, saying to himself he would take the results as the direction he should go in his life. Opening his eyes he saw that he had pointed to the story of a monk of long ago who was so determined to come to awakening that doing zazen late into the night he held an awl at his thigh and would stab himself whenever he was beginning to fall asleep. Through that commitment, he ended up having a deep awakening experience. That story inspired Hakuin to return to his Zen practice and eventually he himself had a deep awakening in which he cried out in realization, "Ganto is alive and well right here now!"

The basic message here is that Ganto was completely one with his dying experience. One could imagine that Ganto was in agony as he was being killed. But in reality, he was not standing outside it.

He was so completely one with the experience,[5] although obviously in physical pain, not getting caught in that. He was free—free to die and to scream completely, totally one with it as he did so. That is the place of no heat or cold. To really understand Ganto you need to put yourself in his place.

Now, if Ganto was truly enlightened, and he was, then what was that scream about? People have this idea that when you have an awakening that means you don't experience suffering. Jacques Lusseyran, after his awakening, was still in Buchenwald and Buchenwald had not changed, but he had. Fully present and engaged with the day-to-day experience of Buchenwald, he was not caught in suffering about it. And yet here Ganto was screaming. In order to solve this koan you need to go where hot and cold kill you, where Ganto is skewered, where any number of other things that are challenging and painful take place.

We don't have to go anywhere special because these challenges occur in our daily lives. They range from little disappointments to devastating sickness and traumas. What was it about Ganto's scream and how do you go beyond heat and cold? How do you go to the place where there is no heat and cold without dissociating or running away from life? You've heard many times of tuning into our body and feeling exactly what the sensations feel like.[6] You abandon ideas about the situation, you simply experience the physical experiences in your body at the time. You become one with whatever is there in that time and that is exactly what Ganto did with the experience of what was going on as he died.

When Roshi Kapleau was at Hosshin-ji, he had gone there a middle-aged businessman with no real physical conditioning. Prior to his arrival there, he had been in Japan for three months living at Nakagawa Soen Roshi's temple where Soen Roshi only required him to sit an hour each day at any time. At the end of those three months, Soen Roshi personally took him up to Obama and translated for him during the Rohatsu sesshin. Of course in America we sit on chairs and back then in Japan they sat on the floor most commonly

---

5 This is not dissociation. Dissociation is trying to escape from an experience by not feeling it. Whereas Ganto was certainly feeling it so completely that it was not a problem.

6 For more instruction on how to do this, look to the book, *Focusing*, by Eugene Gendlin, Bantam Books, 2007.

in a kneeling position. It's quite traditional and certainly was back then that when he was accepted to sit in the zendo at Hosshin-ji, there were only two accepted sitting positions: lotus posture (preferably full lotus posture), or *seiza*. Seiza is sitting on your knees and there are what are known as seiza benches so you can have support under your rear end, which takes pressure off your knees. Here at Mountain Gate you can sit cross-legged or seiza with a seiza bench, or because we sit Rinzai style, facing into the room, you can sit with your feet on the floor as if sitting in a chair. This makes sense in America because most Westerners do not grow up on the floor, we grow up sitting in chairs and there's no point in creating pain.

It was Kapleau's first sesshin ever and as the days went by, he was in increasing physical pain, and fainted the final night of sesshin from the extreme pain. At that point, impressed by his dogged determination, and urging people to stay up all night, somewhere they found a rickety old chair, which they placed in a different room and encouraged his continued efforts with frequent strikes of the kyosaku.[7] Staying on at Hosshin-ji after that Rohatsu sesshin, he joined Daiun Sogaku Harada Roshi in something that was very unusual for the time for Japanese: yoga. By the time he was teaching at the Rochester Zen Center, 12 or 14 years later, he was sitting full lotus without any pain.

As the morning dawned on the final day of that first sesshin, one of the monks, somewhere, was able to get hold of a raw egg (priceless at the time) and brought it to Kapleau to eat. To illustrate how rare that was, when I returned from doing Rohatsu sesshin at Bukkoku-ji many decades later, Roshi Kapleau asked me if I had any tofu during the sesshin. When I said every other day, everyone had a whole cake of tofu, he exclaimed, "A whole cake of tofu?!" He then went on to say that when he was at Hosshin-ji, every two or three months, someone would donate a single cake of tofu to the temple, which of course was divided up among all the monks training there, resulting in each monk getting a very small piece of tofu. The time was post-World War II in Japan where food was scarce and expensive. The temple did not receive enough food to maintain the full health of all the monks.

---

7   Considered the "encouragement stick," the kyosaku is used to strike people on the fleshy part of the shoulders on what is actually an acupuncture point to encourage their ongoing efforts by bringing up energy and grounding them at the same time.

When Kapleau was suffering from malnutrition because of the meager diet at the time, Daiun Roshi sent him to Kamakura to train under Hakuun Yasutani Roshi who had no temple of his own, but had a roving zendo that offered sitting and sesshin in various different locations. In that way, Kapleau could make a living for himself by teaching English, buy food for himself, and continue his intensive training.

Chapter Five
Jump into the 86 Hells

THE GREAT ZEN MASTER HAKUIN teaches us how to deal with fear and anxiety in this chapter as he works with an elderly monk, Zenkai, to become free of his paralyzing fear of going deeper into his zazen. This is a pertinent topic given the prevailing stress in the world today, exacerbated by the extensive COVID-19 crisis, which shook our faith in the stability of our lives. Furthermore, the ongoing political mayhem, mental health crisis, and frequent mass shootings have increased the intense feelings of insecurity. These events consciously or unconsciously bring up a fear of death.

But what really is death? This is a fundamental question that human beings are grappling with whether we realize it or not. For those who find themselves daring to explore what death means, the potential result, if it's gone into thoroughly enough, is profound freedom that can eliminate not only that fear of death but also the fear of life. The ongoing exploration into the nature of death, working with the fear and anxiety that comes up as part of that process, slowly erodes the false sense of who we think we are. That false sense developed over time as a result of our experiences that conditioned us and helped to generate that fear of life. The fear of making mistakes, the fear of not being admired, the fear of being embarrassed, the fear of being wrong, are all actually blows to our assumed identity, which is to say they are a fear of death. Thus, a fear of life is a fear of death.

What is known in Buddhism as the "great death" is the process of seeing through the invented nature of this persona, this false self-image to which we have clung for dear life, not realizing the insubstantiality of it. Seeing through that false self-image is enormously challenging. Like the little man in the Wizard of Oz hiding behind the curtain, we hide behind this mask, not realizing that it is a fake and driving our life in ways that produce pain and suffering. But to see through the mask, to have that curtain removed, initially brings up a frightening sense of vulnerability. Working with that sense of vulnerability, we begin to realize the freedom that comes from not having to be someone that has to be defended, recognized, admired, respected, and so on.

An especially effective way to accomplish this is through committed, ongoing zazen. In our Zen practice, that is what we're doing. In particular, attending sesshin in addition to regular zazen can further speed up that process. Yasutani Roshi said that attending sesshin can be the equivalent of a year of daily Zen practice. However, without that daily ongoing zazen, a sesshin will not be equivalent to a year of practice. Sesshin, of course, being a period normally of seven days when we have set aside this very precious time in which to concentrate fully on that mission. We're called upon to do it because there's something within us that deeply needs to know, deeply yearns to become free. Essential is the faith that we can do it. And we can do it. Doing so will result in genuine freedom and the ability to live an authentic life.

In our Zen practice, there is the supportive environment of sitting in the zendo with fellow, committed sangha members, and the support naturally offered there in that environment. There are also tools to help us successfully navigate and deepen our Zen practice: the extended outbreath (susok'kan), koans, inspiration from teisho, the examples of fellow sangha members, work practice (samu), and guidance from our teacher. Sitting together in a zendo is normally more powerful than sitting alone in our home environment where the habit energies of being in that environment can distract us from our practice. In particular, the extended outbreath is an unusually powerful tool. We can work on it day after day, and gradually go deeper and open more to that Truth.

As much as we want indications of progress, especially in our earlier years of practice, there are no obvious milestones. Unlike being in school where there are periodic exams that affirm our advancement, there are no such landmarks. Nor is it like driving along the highway noting the miles drop away as you reach closer to your destination. That is probably the biggest challenge in our earlier years of Zen practice. And the fundamental benefit, curiously enough, at this point in our practice is that there are no signs that you're going forward or backwards. Generally, we have little to go on except faith, support of the sangha, the encouragement of our teacher, and eventually recognizing the positive but subtle results accruing from that Zen practice.

I can remember going through a period of urgently needing affirmation that my practice was working and I was going in the right direction. I went to one of my fellow sangha members who had in the months before been passed on his breakthrough koan[1] and expressed my anxiety. I will never forget what he said: "Don't worry, Zen practice is cumulative." What he meant by that is that all our zazen that may seem to be accomplishing nothing as we continue to struggle with our habitual patterns of mind is gradually making it possible to come to awakening. We may have the idea that plopping down on a cushion for a few minutes is going to open us to satori. Eventually it will if we persist, but as part of that process we will have to work through what is preventing us from recognizing that deep Truth.

Hakuin spoke metaphorically of this during his evening encouragement talk on the second night of a *Rohatsu* Sesshin when he said,

> Anywhere people engage in a practice of the Way, protecting deities and obstructing deities are also present. It is like crowds gathering in towns and cities and drawing thieves there as well. When a student's mind is focused firmly in the great vow of universal salvation, the protecting deities gain strength. But when the mind begins to waver and impede itself, it is obstructing deities who strengthen.

---

1   In a map of Rinzai Zen practice, one starts with the extended outbreath and as that works its magic, still using the susok'kan, you start working on a breakthrough koan. There are several traditional breakthrough koans, the most well known one being the koan, "Mu." Other breakthrough koans include, "What is the sound of one hand," "Show me your face before your parents were born," and the modern version of these, "Who am I?" One works on these breakthrough koans, generally for many years. The work on those koans gradually deepens our understanding of reality and eventually reveals a great enough depth of understanding that our teacher allows us to work through the extended curriculum of subsequent koans in order to continue to clarify and broaden that understanding.

It is thus absolutely essential that you begin your practice by arousing the great Bodhisattva vow, focusing your mind with selfless humility on the suffering of sentient beings, rooting it in the fervent prayer that each and every one of them reach the deliverance of enlightenment.[2] No one has ever attained full realization of the great Way of the Buddhas who was not inspired by the power of this vow.

It is like the practice of archery. You won't hit the center of the target the first or second time you shoot an arrow. But in time, if you continue to practice diligently, you are sure to grasp the knack. In practicing Zen, it is the same.[3]

What seems to be an apparent forward and backward movement in our practice can, on occasion, bring up a compelling need to have our progress clearly recognized. If that is not forthcoming, it doesn't mean we haven't made progress. Instead it means we have an opportunity to work with yet another place we're caught in attempting to reinforce that self-image. This is why it's so vital to work with a teacher. And because a teacher has been there ahead of you and has worked through these very same things guided by their teacher, and consequently has a clear perception of when a person is going in the right direction and can encourage and guide, sometimes saying nothing. A teacher is just one who has been there, a little bit ahead of each one of us, and that has its benefits.

Hakuin also said, "The *Shurangama Sutra* says that when a person returns to Truth in the attainment of the Way, everything in all the ten directions, including empty space itself, vanishes without a trace." That refers to a very deep samadhi, a precursor for coming to awakening. That is not to say one deep samadhi will necessarily result in immediate awakening right then. As well, there are various

---

2   Unlike in Japan where the culture focuses on the group rather than the individual, in our individualistic Western cultures most people would be intent on relieving their own suffering more than the suffering of everyone.

3   From Hakuin's *Rohatsu Exhortations*, unpublished and privately shared by Norman Waddell.

different levels of samadhi. For example, becoming so absorbed in a movie that we become the movie. The same can be said these days of video games. Playing a sport is another example, as is rock climbing, which requires such focus that an individual becomes one with the unfolding experience. Being in the midst of a rock concert where one loses oneself in the surging energy of the crowd is a milder example. But these are more superficial levels of samadhi and normally do not lead to awakening. However, the sense of freedom that is there during these experiences is often addictive. This is because all human beings yearn to return to their True Home.

Living invested in the self-image is painful because our sense of being a decent human being, capable and kind, is periodically challenged when we get a low grade on an exam, when somebody gets angry at us, when we get embarrassed. But until we can see deeply enough through the falsity of it, we're stuck in that purgatory of dissatisfaction and pain. If our samadhi is deep enough that in those hours we die to our persona, emerging from that profound state into awakening, we realize, as Harada Roshi put it, "All I need to do is receive, is simply to receive." In other words, we no longer need to defend, no longer need to rationalize; clarity simply arises to respond in a way that is appropriate in each arising circumstance. The anxiety that accompanies those previously felt needs will recede and eventually with the long maturation disappear completely. When we emerge from that samadhi and come back to life again, it is different. Something has let go.

It's also a point in our practice where a great fear can come up ahead of that, because if we let go, if we disappear, are we going to be able to come back? Or are we going to disappear permanently? Will we no longer be? The Great Death is the clear seeing through of our false persona into the reality of who we really are and the freedom that has always been there if we don't lock ourselves into the rigidity of being somebody and the subsequent need to defend that persona. Thus there are periods of time as our practice continues where fear comes up. That fear indicates the fixed sense of who we are begins to seem less real as our zazen gradually deepens. This is an especially challenging time for practitioners because it is so tempting to assume that that fear means the practice is not working and so we're tempted to quit.

Roshi Kapleau, when he was training at Hosshin-ji, spoke of wanting to flee many times. At one point he got so far as the front door with his bags packed, when, in his words, "I came to my senses," and returned to committed practice at the monastery. After his stint as a court reporter during the war crimes trials in Japan, and being exposed to the peace he experienced in the gardens of Japanese temples, he had decided to return to Japan for authentic Zen training. He had "burned all his bridges" in the United States and had nothing to return to. Recognizing that helped him stay the course in his practice. Not many people come to Zen practice because they have a sense that there's no alternative, but for those who do, it's of great advantage at times like this. That recognition will also support people in their commitment to continue with post-satori practice and the long maturation. Without that continuing practice, that awakening will gradually fade as we slowly return to a growing investment in a self-image. We can also fall into a purgatory, which is what Zenkai did.

The elderly monk, Zenkai, had decades before had some level of kensho, but lacking access to a teacher to help him deepen it and work on the long maturation, he ended up falling prey to a fear of going deeper. For several decades, he languished in this state of anxiety before finally coming to see Hakuin for help. Now let's get into what Hakuin says about jumping into the 86 hells.[4] "In the Shōtoku era (1711–15) there was a priest in Edo [modern day Tokyo] who called himself Zenkai... He began his Zen practice at the age of twenty-three and experienced a *kenshō*." For anyone, following a kensho, it is vital to continue working with a teacher and work through post-satori practice, which includes the long maturation.

Post-satori practice is absolutely essential, but Zenkai, lacking a teacher, did not understand the need for that. Hakuin continues, "But he lamented how difficult it still was for him to control the workings of his mind. He decided to enter the mountains of Kumano on the Kii peninsula, cut himself off from the outside world, and devote himself to an austere training regimen." This is a dangerous move, though many people may be drawn to it out of relief from the

---

4   For the full account, see pages 452-455 in *Poison Blossoms from a Thicket of Thorn* by Hakuin Zenji and translated by Norman Waddell.

seeming pressure of working with a teacher, but it is self-defeating. Without a guide, despite a kensho, we can settle into a self-designed practice that will lead to nowhere as Zenkai did.

> On his way he passed through Awano and Mino province, thinking to stop for a while with several priests of his acquaintance who were residing there. Meeting Zenkai and seeing the strength he had attained in his pursuit of the Way, his friends were more than glad to take him in when he arrived. But they were dismayed when they heard of his plan to proceed into the forests of Kumano. They urged him to find a quiet hermitage in Mino. Zenkai agreed, and gave up his idea of going to Kumano altogether.
>
> It is a thousand pities that because a student fails to encounter a genuine teacher at the beginning of his training and remains ignorant of the practice that continues after satori, he will delight in immersing himself in the pure existence of this kind, cut off from the world. Engaged in such profitless silent meditation, he focuses intently on ridding his mind of thoughts.

Given the traditional Japanese admonition to "cut your thoughts," we can be led to assume that we are supposed to stop thinking. But, in reality, that admonition actually means not to get rid of thoughts but to cut our attachments to thoughts. Clearly, Zenkai misunderstood this. When we focus deeply, thoughts naturally diminish.

> For forty years Zenkai continued to reside in the hermitage he built in Mino. With growing age, his resolve began to falter. His heart grew weary. He found that the more he tried to sweep thoughts from his mind, the more confused his mind became. Although having lived to a considerable age as a Buddhist priest, as death approached his fears of the

sufferings that lay ahead in the next world remained. He began quietly to recite the Nembutsu."[5] When in time he came to regard this as a rather roundabout way of reaching awakening, he started repeating his own name instead, "Zenkai, Zenkai," over and over.

Where had the original attainment he'd experienced as a young monk gone? Now his nights were plagued by bad dreams, his days tormented by troubling thoughts. He visited various Buddhist teachers seeking their advice on how to break through this impasse. They told him he was suffering from "Zen sickness" and could offer him no help. He took to moping about doing zazen with tears in his eyes.

One priest, feeling pity for him, said, "Why don't you go to Suruga province and see Master Kokurin [Hakuin]. I'm sure he will be able to help you."

With considerable difficulty owing into his great age, the priest made his way to my temple in Suruga and earnestly requested an interview. The monk who received him came to my chambers with a smile on his face. "A grubby old priest with a broken-down old pilgrim's case on his back just showed up," he reported. "His hair is tangled like a mugwort ball, he has a filthy face, and his robe and sedge hat are in tatters. He requested an interview with you in the gruff accent of the Bandō region. Will you see him?"

I said, "Tell him I'm sick. Give him something to eat and then send him on his way." Then I heard a voice shouting loudly from outside the gate, "I'm an old man. I'm over eighty years old. I had a very long trip to come here. Are you going to pretend you're sick and just send me away? Where is your compassion?" I had little choice but to grant his request. He

---

[5] Recitation of the Nembutsu, "I place my faith in Amida Buddha," is a Pure Land practice, not a Zen practice.

came into my chambers. "I suffered for years from Zen sickness," he blustered. "Please, master, in your great compassion, do something for me. Help me!"

"Tell me about your Zen sickness —what is it like?" I asked.

"I'm troubled by thoughts in the daytime. At night I have dreams," he replied.

"Do you know what is having those troubling thoughts?" I asked.

"Stop, please. I can't bear to think about emptiness," he said.

"What's wrong with thinking about emptiness?" I asked.

"If a person attaches to emptiness, he will surely fall into hell."

"Come a little closer. I'm going to free you from your suffering."

"I'm certainly glad to hear that," he said, and drew towards me.

"Do you know how many hells exist for someone attached to emptiness?" I asked him.

"No, I don't know that," he replied.

"There at eighty-six. I want you to go down into hell right now and distribute yourself among all 86."

Wordless the priest stared pie-eyed at me.

"Come on! Get down into them!"

"Priests are supposed to save you from hell. What kind of teacher would try to send a student there?" he cried.

"You say you're from Kantō, but it seems you've never heard what Suzuki Shōsan said: 'The direct, rough-hewn spirit of Kantō is very close to Zen.' If you were really a Kantō priest, you should be able to jump into hell without a second thought."

"Could you?" he said.

"Get down there and explore these hells, one by one! There's not a single hell I haven't fallen into!"

He abruptly prostrated himself before me. His eyes filled with tears. "What a great and wonderful teacher you are, master Hakuin," he said. "Your compassion has liberated me. Allowed me to break completely free from my delusions. I feel as though I have suddenly awakened from a terrible dream. There's no way I can describe the joy I now feel!" He prostrated himself 20 or 30 times, crying and laughing all the while. He then left, returned to the guests' quarters, latched the door shut and went to sleep.

The next morning Zenkai approached me with a broad smile on his face. I asked him whether he had seen any bad dreams during the night. "I hadn't enjoyed a sound sleep for over 40 years," he said. "But last night I slept like a log. It is the difference between a mediocre physician, who always doles out the same medicine to his patients, and a great one, who prescribes a purgative at just the right time. If you had not applied that purgative just when you did, how could you have saved me from that terrible sickness?"

When he finished speaking, he performed I don't know how many prostrations before me. I myself was overcome with joy.

The real message here is to walk right into the bodily feeling, meaning energy of the mind state, whatever the mind state seems to be. Be curious about it. Open to it. Even if it's a terrible feeling, even if it's great fear, walk in as far as you can. When it gets to be almost too much back out. And then later walk back in again. Open increasingly and as you continue this practice going into those 86 hells, one by one, you will find that little by little any fear of hell dissolves. And little by little you will become free, so that it won't matter what mind state comes forth. And actually, what happens then is like what happened to old Zenkai. The mind states won't come forth. They'll diminish in power and eventually some of them will just simply disappear and not arise anymore. Others will become a shadow of themselves. Continue, and more of them will do the same. The only way to become free is not to turn your back on what you're fearing or what you're caught in. But to feel the bodily energy of what that mind state feels like. To stay out of the stories. Because stories can't do anything in terms of releasing you from suffering. If you have experienced trauma, however, it's important to work with a trained trauma therapist to assist with this process.

Chapter Six
Zen Practice and Suppression of Feelings

This chapter explores the dangers of using Zen practice to suppress difficult feelings. Human beings are psychological creatures and we have issues. We grow up in different kinds of environments, some of them not so happy and some of them downright traumatic. In general, children go through periods of anger as they learn how to live in the world. There are, for example, what are known as the "terrible twos" and often as we learn to navigate the world there are other instances in our younger years in which we get angry. Unless we have enlightened parents, the adults around us don't understand how to work with anger and usually can't do more than say "Stop that! Don't be angry!" without giving us any way to do so. Wanting to be good kids, the only thing we can think to do is shut it down by suppressing it or storming out of the room and throwing something.

There was a period of time, back in the '80s, where psychotherapists thought that screaming or punching pillows was an appropriate way to deal with anger. This was a popular psychotherapeutic tool until it became clear that, even though it momentarily relieved anger, it only reinforced it, at the time leaving us no alternative but to suppress it. This is a practice which can seemingly remove it from our consciousness, but actually raises our blood pressure and has other negative physiological side effects. As well, even if we don't "feel angry" that anger is felt by the people around us. So, nothing's solved.

We experience loss and other forms of pain and suffering, sometimes at the hands of our caregivers, sometimes simply from the circumstances of our lives, and they all impact us. Many people take up meditation as an escape from feeling the pain of those experiences. It's important to recognize, as you read in the previous chapter, that meditation is not meant to be an escape. It's meant to gradually open us to the freedom to truly be at one with whatever is going on, regardless of how it is. If what is going on is traumatic, it's essential to also engage the specialized help of an experienced trauma therapist to work with the trauma itself.1 As the Christian serenity prayer reads, "God grant me the serenity to accept the things I cannot change, the courage to change the things I can, and the wisdom to know the difference."[2]

Over the decades, there have been reports of abuses by Buddhist teachers regardless of type of Buddhism.[3] When Buddhist practice is not gone thoroughly, deeply, and widely enough, in other words, if it has a narrow focus such as with the admonition in Zen "just 'Mu'!" significant conditioning can remain unaddressed. In practicing entirely according to this dictum, ignoring post-satori practice and the long maturation, it is easy to use the practice to cover up or ignore parts of our conditioning that really need to be worked through and which can keep us caught in dysfunctional behavior. When one is using the meditation practice to cover up or avoid pain or discomfort, that dysfunction remains uncorrected. But the further danger in using practice to suppress naturally prevents one from being able to work with those difficult mind states or experiences and eventually become free of them.

To give cultural and historical background to the suppression of feelings within Buddhist practice, the religion began in India more than 2500 years ago, then spread to Southeast Asian countries where, except for Vietnam, it took Theravadin form. Then it made its way to China, Korea, Central Asia, Vietnam, Japan, and eventually to America and the West in the Mahayana form. Much of the Zen practice in the United States has come to us directly from

---

1   These days, there are some truly effective trauma therapists; there are also some who could use a little more experience. Ideally, the trauma therapist you would find an affinity with is also someone who would be doing meditation.

2   Christianity, Judaism, and Islam posit an all-powerful god who creates human beings and everything else in this world. I; in Buddhism, this is seen as a rich "field" or "plane" of energetic potentiality from which, when karma ripens, energy coalesces and things and beings (including people) emerge as seeming individuals. When that karma begins to dissolve, these concentrations of energy that form all beings and things separate. We cannot say "return to that plane of potentiality" because in reality nothing has ever left it.

3   This type of behavior is not limited to Buddhism. Psychiatrists, psychologists, doctors, teachers, ministers, politicians, and priests of many different faiths have all been found guilty of this misconduct.

Zen Practice and the Suppression of Feelings

Japan, which is quite culturally different from America. The most important difference is that Japanese culture is steeped in focus and concern for the group over the individual. Accordingly, the person is focused on serving the group, not serving themselves, hence there is rarely anything to suppress. Within Japanese culture, many things are naturally understood without having to be specified.

On the other hand, American culture focuses on the individual over the group; Americans are accustomed to being instructed in detail and not expected to have an implicit cultural understanding of what they are to do. As a result, the way Zen practice grew in Japan is especially effective in the Japanese culture but is, when taken literally, not as effective in the more individualistic American culture. Although in Japan in the 18th Century Hakuin mentioned the need for post-satori practice and the long maturation, and his Dharma successor Torei Enji emphasized it, it's not normally spoken of these days in Japanese Zen, and the emphasis did not cross over in the transfer to Western Zen. Here and there, some Western Zen teachers recognize the need for an expanded view of Zen practice, and Norman Waddell's translations of the writings of Hakuin have also opened our eyes to this.

As we grow from infancy to adulthood and onward, our experiences condition us and we live out of that conditioning, which creates expectations of the world we live in, our role in it, whether we can trust situations or people, and whether we feel safe or not. There are many events in our lives that can create that conditioning. For example, whether we were loved and embraced and supported and felt safe as we were growing up, versus if we were ignored and our needs were not met and we felt unsafe, or worse, if we experienced abuse. All of these experiences created a persona that defined how we interacted with the world. Often when we experience trauma, we may block it from consciousness. If we grow up in isolated circumstances, we may not recognize that our painful growing up was not normal.

As we begin Zen practice, at first things go along seemingly well because we're in the "honeymoon" period—the excitement of learning something new that has promises of freedom and happiness. But then as we get deeper in Zen practice those underlying experiences may begin to rise to the surface of consciousness. At this point, we're offered the opportunity to work with those experiences through the felt-sense within our zazen and perhaps engage in services of a trained psychotherapist. But if we choose to override them, we will both limit our Zen practice and keep ourselves trapped, preventing the liberation that Zen practice offers. In the previous chapter, when Zenkai chose to go off on his own and practice without the guidance of a teacher he was doing exactly that. As you could see, it became increasingly difficult until he met Hakuin and Hakuin helped him liberate himself by urging Zenkai to "jump into the 86 hells," a metaphor for feeling fully into those fears.

We may not necessarily have experienced trauma, but our personalities, even after enlightenment, can still be a little rough. If we choose not to engage in the long maturation, we will have lost the opportunity to soften and ease that roughness. Our behavior won't necessarily change and the more challenging aspects of our personality continue to cause pain and suffering. Recalling the koans featuring Tokusan in a previous chapter, had he not engaged in post-satori practice and the long maturation, Tokusan would not have, later in his life, been able to return to his quarters without irritation or resistance and to wait until the meal gong was rung. Some may feel the term "radical acceptance" applies to this situation. Radical acceptance is about offering an uncomfortable feeling acceptance even though you may not like it. However, at this point in his life, Tokusan was truly free and so simply returned to his room to wait. The common assumption that enlightenment experience will bring us home free is not necessarily accurate. However, a kensho experience will definitely make the long maturation easier, for we won't be as attached to a persona that has habitual patterns of behavior as we were prior to that kensho. Nonetheless, the work of the long maturation is essential if we are to become truly free, including free of creating suffering. The long maturation can begin way before any kind of kensho; it can begin the moment you step foot into the zendo, or sit down on the cushion, because it goes hand in hand with deepening Zen practice.

At Hidden Valley Zen Center in San Marcos, California there is a scroll that reads, "Though the eight winds may blow, It is not disturbed." What are these "eight winds" and what is "It"? To quote the Myoshin-ji[4] website[5] "The 'eight winds' are eight influences that agitate and inflame the human heart and mind. They consist of four favorable circumstances (prosperity, honor, praise, and pleasure) and four setbacks (decline, disgrace, censure and suffering.)" And "It" refers to our true nature. How can we work with our reactions to those metaphorical eight winds and live from that "It"? It's not about shutting ourselves down and practicing above the radar in a mind state of what is really dissociation and assuming that is good Zen practice. In a word, it is committed zazen under the guidance of a true teacher, with patience and likely for a very long time. In some cases, that teacher might recommend working with a therapist to help clear up certain psychological blocks. Psychotherapy and Zen can often speed up the work of Zen practice.

In my own case, I had experienced trauma while still young and had suppressed the terror that had arisen as a result of that, although it did come up in nightmares. It was an extreme terror impossible to describe, and in order to function in the world I had had to suppress it. Many years later, I began Zen practice and after two and a half years of practicing on my own was accepted to live and train at the Rochester Zen Center. After attending a four-day sesshin, I moved to Rochester and attended my first seven-day sesshin. It was not until eight months later that a space became available for me to live and train at the Rochester Zen Center. In the meantime, I survived on my own but attended the Center for every single sitting. At one time, one of the other sangha members living there, when I asked him some questions because I was in psychic pain, commented "I believe you've repressed some important things." This man was a trained psychiatrist who was taking a leave of absence to work on his own Zen practice, but it was too early for me to "get" what he was talking about. I did notice, however, that I was having frequent headaches until one day I realized that I wasn't having frequent headaches, I was having spaces within the ongoing relentless headache I had had for so long that it became unnoticeable until there were gaps in it.

Some years later, I began psychotherapy with a family systems

---

4   One of the major headquarter temples of the Rinzai sect.

5   www.nstmyoshinji.org

therapist, through which I explored the relationships among generations of my family to see how certain behavior patterns were passed down. It was somewhat helpful. But it wasn't until I was advanced enough that I was assigned to be, for the first time, the second monitor for a sesshin that I had no choice but to get into a deeper form of therapy.[6] By that time my blood pressure had become so high that I was ordered by my doctor to do aerobic exercise daily. During the exercise period each day of sesshin I was permitted to run around in the garden of the Rochester Zen Center while everyone else did a very slow form of yoga in the Buddha Hall. I had an excruciating headache and began to imagine that the headache was caused by a head full of big, heavy railroad spikes. I imagined pulling them out one at a time. Each time I pulled a spike out, the headache in that part of my head was relieved. But by the time I removed all the spikes from my head, I found myself, in my imagination, holding a whole pile of those spikes that were so toxic there was no safe place in the universe to put them.

The Monday morning as soon as sesshin ended, I made an appointment with a PhD clinical psychologist who had been a member of the Rochester Zen Center for many years. She skillfully helped me to begin freeing myself from the effects of the trauma of my childhood. At one point during a therapy session, I doubled over in anguish as the full impact of feelings of abandonment I had suppressed since infancy hit me. It was too soon, however, to open to the terror I'd also been living with because of incidents that had happened in my later childhood and the reminders of those incidents. From the time I was eight, I had a real reason to fear for my life at the hands of my mother. I was pointedly reminded of this until I finally left home during my second year in college. The terror was so strong, still many years later, that I could not spend more than two or three nights in any house my parents were living in at the time. Even after she died, it was the same. After she died, I began having nightmares of having to kill somebody before they killed me.

---

6   In Roshi Kapleau's efforts to make Zen more palatable to Americans, he translated the names of what are now known in America as the "officers" of a Zen Center or Temple from "jikijitsu," "jishario," "tenzo," "densu," and "fusui." Jikijitsu and jishario became the first and second monitors. He also translated a number of chants into English. After so many years of living in Japan, he was fluent in Japanese. His translations also include the Four Bodhisattva Vows, the Jukai Ceremony, and Bodhisattva Precepts.

There was no question they wanted to kill me, but I didn't want to kill anybody. When I described the nightmare to my therapist, mentioning that after several nights of struggling with not wanting to kill someone but feeling an urge that I had to in order to survive. I finally saw the woman who was the one who wanted to kill me. She was lying down and I forced myself to try to hit her mildly on her leg with my purse in a ridiculous attempt to kill her, all the while knowing it wouldn't. I was surprised as she just lay there and smiled at me. When I mentioned that last encounter to my therapist, especially my surprise at the smile, she asked, "Do you suppose she was smiling because she was dead?" It hit me that the abandonment of my early years, the rage against me in my later years, were all attempts of her trying to deny my existence. By then, further intense work in therapy and Zen practice had finally freed me of the hold it had on my life and the need to suppress feeling that terror. I share this story because it is my earnest hope that all of you can recognize that whatever your history is, you can become free.

I also learned through an experience in a sesshin during one of the extended periods in Mexico with Roshi Kapleau that it is impossible to shut down one part of your mind and keep the other part open enough to do Zen practice. By then I had worked well into the subsequent koans and at that particular sesshin, somehow, I couldn't answer the koan. Days went by and finally Roshi said to me, "I don't know what's going on but normally you would have been able to answer this koan at least a couple of days ago." Suddenly I realized what the problem was. Some circumstances that took place just before sesshin had hit on old abandonment issues and brought up anger which I had shut down. Because I had suppressed that anger, I was unable to function freely enough to answer the koan. Once I realized what I had done and allowed myself to feel again, I passed that koan soon after, and several other koans in that sesshin. It drove home the importance of not suppressing anything if you're to practice effectively and ultimately live a free life.

Chapter Seven
Unweaving the Tapestry, Exploring the Mind

THE TRUE MIND OF THE TATHAGATA is no other than our own mind even though the Tathagata, which is the name the Buddha used to refer to himself, lived more than 2500 years ago. How can that be? "The Original Face before our parents were born,"[1] is the very same experience as the Tathagata despite the difference in time and space. It is the same Face, the same essence, the undying, unborn essence of who we are. What prevents us from readily experiencing it is a complex weaving developed at least since birth. This weaving becomes increasingly dense, making it difficult to recognize. What blinds us to our Original Face is the creation of that tapestry consisting of beliefs, assumptions, ideas, and conditioning that we have. In order to experience that Original Face we will need to work our way into unweaving the tapestry we have developed as our life has progressed.

Although initially we are clueless as to how to go about this process of uncovering our Original Face and are still caught in our analytical mind as we struggle to make sense of it, at some point we learn that it is not about analysis. It is not about using our intellect to open to that Original Face. That search cannot be done through words, but we must sense our way deeper into the search. Once we recognize that, the bite of anxiety of not succeeding analytically begins to ease and, now with a better sense of how to go about it, the search becomes exciting. We can really cut to the chase if we tune in from the very beginning.

What do we mean by "tune in"? In the early 1980s, a philosopher, Eugene Gendlin, who worked more in psychology than philosophy, was part of a research project to determine the difference between patients able to quickly transform through therapy while others could take months or years without progress. It was quickly

---
1   One of the "breakthrough" koans.

discovered that the ones who could proceed effectively in their therapy were able to do something called "tuning in to the felt-sense," meaning the physical sense of energy in their body rather than abstract analysis. The results of the research were so clear that Eugene Gendlin wrote a book describing how to open to the felt-sense.[2]

In searching for Mu, the sound of one hand, or your Original Face, don't try to get somewhere to some *thing* because there's no somewhere to go and no something to get to. It's all here in this very moment and there's nowhere else it could be. This is not so easy to grasp. Tokusan —mentioned in a previous chapter—had originally been famous for his study of the Vinaya (the rules for monks and nuns) and later for his analytical study and writings on the *Diamond Sutra*. Incensed at hearing that experiential Zen was being taught in the south, he headed down there to correct what he saw as wrong.[3] He encountered in his travels an old woman selling cakes known in the era as "mind refreshers" from a roadside stand. He stopped to buy one of those cakes and the woman asked him what was in his backpack, to which he proudly answered, "My commentaries on the *Diamond Sutra*." In response, she sweetly asked, "in the *Diamond Sutra* it says 'future mind cannot be found, past mind cannot be found, present mind cannot be found. Which mind would you like to refresh? If you can answer I will give you one of these mind-refreshers." This flummoxed Tokusan and changed the purpose of his journey. He asked the woman if there was a teacher nearby. He was told of Zen master Ryutan and so went there to enter the master's forge.[4] Eventually, Tokusan burned all his research and teachings on the *Diamond Sutra* and as you learned in a previous chapter became a deeply enlightened Zen teacher.

I'd like to share with you some of the words of Huang Po who is known in Japanese as Obaku, teacher of Rinzai. He was a rather imposing looking person. He was quite tall and supposedly had a forehead with a big lump on the front of it. Some said the lump

---

2   *Focusing* by Eugene Gendlin, Bantam books, 2007.

3   Far into the advanced practice of working on subsequent koans one does begin to read certain sutras experientially as a way to broaden and deepen one's practice.

4   There are many references in Zen to "entering the master's forge" such as "without entering the master's forge many times, how can pure gold be revealed?" This translates to mean without the challenges of serious Zen training, how can one's true nature be revealed?

arose because he did so many prostrations. At any rate, he was very deeply realized and here he's pointing at what was said at the beginning of this chapter, "All Buddhas and all ordinary beings are nothing but the one mind. This mind is beginningless and endless, unborn and indestructible. It has no color or shape, neither exists nor doesn't exist, isn't old or new, long or short, large or small, since it transcends all measures, limits names, and comparisons. It is what you see in front of you. Start to think about it and immediately you are mistaken."

The *Prajna Paramita*, the *Heart of Perfect Wisdom*, which is considered the most advanced teaching of the Buddha, in essence is saying the same thing. "No eye, ear, nose, tongue, body, mind, no color, sound, smell, taste, touch, or what the mind takes hold of, nor even act of sensing, no ignorance nor end of it." How can there be no ignorance and yet no end of ignorance? This really was my first koan even though theoretically I was working on Mu. Mu, I had no particular connection to. How can form be empty? How come this table which is certainly solid is also empty at the same time? This really grabbed me. It's a deep level of understanding when you are able to experience that as the truth. And when you experience that as the truth then you become quite a bit freer.

It's not something, as Tokusan learned from that old woman, that can be thought about or understood through analysis. However, the way to open to that understanding is to explore beyond words, is to reach beyond words, open to the possibility that the understanding will make itself known. When we do the extended out breath, for example, we're not thinking our way down the breath; we're experiencing our way down the breath with curiosity and with an openness to that possibility. In other words, when we are breathing out, we simply breathe out, but there is stuff going on in our body, there is perception. What is that perception? What are those sensations? If we feel discomfort or restlessness in our body then it's important to tune in to those sensations and let them reveal to us what is causing them. When we offer these uncomfortable sensations radical acceptance suddenly there is space and we feel less compelled to escape those sensations. You don't have to escape into analysis or writing the Great American Novel about it.

For example, where's the one that is feeling that experience? And is that experience saying something? Of course not in words, but we communicate in many, many different ways and words are an extremely limited form of communication. In Japan one admired aspect of a conversation is when two people are talking and they finish each other's sentences. It's considered very positive and an indication of the deep presence and clear understanding between the two people talking. It is also considered a sign of respect. Whereas in America if you complete someone else's sentence, it's seen as an insult and an act of aggression: "hurry up and finish what you're saying!"

In Zen practice we need to learn to adopt the Japanese way of communication through total presence and the accurate sensing that can come through that presence and to leave thoughts, ideas, and analysis out of the search. Such clear and aware presence is a most important aspect of living an enlightened life and it is important to develop it increasingly fully through our Zen meditation. Relatively early in my practice, when I was still working on the koan Mu, during kinhin, I noticed that Gordy Bruen, a fellow student, was still seated on the tan, totally absorbed. He remained so throughout the sesshin. I learned later that he had had a kensho during that sesshin. He exclaimed to me afterwards, "Why didn't someone tell me it's about exploring your own mind?!" Of course that means wordlessly exploring the experience, the whole rich and deep experience of consciousness.

But contrary to this way of working, we try to create a mind of what we think enlightenment is, which of course is not an enlightened mind. What is required instead is to continue unweaving the tapestry of conditioning that has long obscured that enlightened mind. Deep, concentrated, committed Zen practice, working with an authentic Zen teacher and perhaps also with the help of an appropriate therapist[5] is the way to experience success. It needs to be recognized that this will not be accomplished quickly, so be prepared for remaining in for the long haul if you truly want to become free.

---

5   It is recognized these days that Peter Levine's "somatic experiencing" is one of the most effective ways of working with all manner of psychological blocks including trauma.

Let go and explore. Let yourself fall into the moment's experience. Of course notice when you're resistant to it, notice when you may have positive or negative feelings about it, but don't go there, just notice, and keep reaching deeper, keep exploring more completely. It's a little like having this amazing, complex tapestry that is your own mind and what you're doing is gradually unweaving it and seeing what's beyond, what's beneath. Through that, over time, we begin to see where we're caught in what we're calling attachments, clinging, where we want things to be a certain way, where we don't want things to be a certain way, where we want to be recognized, where we want to be admired, where we don't want to be told what to do, when we don't want to be told that what we're doing is not as helpful as it could be, all of those kinds of things. Through remaining present with the physical experience of these sensations, the identification of which we just named, we can become more and more free and eventually experience our True Self.[6]

There's a member here who many years ago was with a friend and they were out in the deep forest and they were so interested in what they were doing that they didn't notice it was getting dark and there was no moon that night to guide them back to their truck. But, they turned around and felt their way back, not reaching out and touching trees, but sensing. They had walked along a stream, there was no path, and there were low hanging branches, as well as fallen branches and rocks on the ground. But sensing each one of these, these tall men neither stumbled nor hit their heads on any low hanging branches though it was pitch dark. Asked about how they got back to their truck, they responded "We don't know. We sensed where objects that would have impeded us were."

Not long ago, there was an experiment in which a blind man was asked to walk down a long hallway littered with various boxes and other objects. He was able to walk down the entire length of the hallway without bumping into the objects that were in his path. Jacques Lusseyran, whom you've met in previous chapters and in Book One of *Deepening Zen: The Long Maturation* learned very early on, soon after he was blinded at age eight, that if he were angry,

---

6   Mu, sound of one hand, the Face before our parents were born.

jealous, or otherwise upset, he would bump into furniture in his house. But if he was not in those mind states, he was able to freely move around without bumping into anything. Moreover, outdoors he could sense the height of walls and trees nearby and the distance between himself and those objects. Blind or sighted, we all have that ability, but like Jacques when he was in a distracted mind state, we in our nearly perennial mind states have difficulty perceiving beyond our normal habitual perceptions. What is essential in the process of unweaving that tapestry is the ability to sense beyond our usual perceptions.

This is spoken of in many ways by many of the teachers of the past. Suzuki Roshi called this inherent ability "beginner's mind." The Korean Seon teacher, Seung Sahn Sunim, called it "only don't know." When we walk into an experience with no preconceived ideas about it but a willingness to be open to the experience, it's quite amazing what can happen. If you're truly present with anything, it's three-dimensional, rich, and fulfilling no matter what it is. There's an expression in Zen, "even garbage glitters like gold." So, it is only that we have ideas about what we are, what we have to have to be happy or fulfilled, whether we're happy or unhappy, whether we like our situation or not. It's only because of those that we are caught in suffering, basically, in fear, in anxiety, in anger, in sadness. This doesn't mean there are not things to be sad or angry about, but you'll see it differently and you'll be able to work with it differently as you begin to unweave the tapestry.

Chapter Eight
Benefits of Being Honed by Life and Zen Practice

APRIL FOOL'S DAY, in America, is a day of fun and light hearted jokes. So it was at the Rochester Zen Center every year. In this particular year on April first we were not in sesshin and so the hijinks were on full display. Outside of sesshin, Sunday mornings were dedicated to zazen and a teisho by the teacher. Being April first—April Fool's Day—Bodhin Roshi would be giving a humorous talk that would bring forth gales of laughter in the zendo. Normally the day would begin with a wake-up bell. Zazen would precede the teisho on Sunday mornings and to alert people fifteen minutes before there would be three strikes on the big bell that hung on the landing outside the zendo. At five minutes before the teisho the han would be struck and Bodhin Roshi would enter the zendo and take his seat on the *tan*[1] facing the altar. The lectern would be moved forward to a convenient space for him, he would be presented with his *katsu* and then water in his ceramic cup with a lid. He would commence his teisho, at the end of which the Bodhisattva Vows would be chanted, he would exit the zendo, followed by everyone else where they would gather in the dining room for bagels and tea. This typical post-teisho Sunday morning brunch was also a time for enjoying the company of fellow sangha members.

But on this particular April first there were no holds barred. The first prank unfolded when Pirko-Lisa, an RZC resident who was scheduled to ring the wake-up bell, discovered that the clapper had been taken out of the bell. Having no other choice, she roamed the halls calling out "ga-ding! ga-ding! ga-ding!" followed by a few chuckles. When Sante Poromaa, another RZC resident, went to strike the fifteen-minute warning bell, instead of the usual deep, resonant sound, there was a sudden "thunk," then ripples of laughter from the zendo. It seemed that someone had stuffed a *zafu* up

---

1 The sitting platform typical in traditional Zen temples, whether in Japan or the United States.

inside the bell. Somehow the pranksters overlooked the *han* and so the riff was properly played five minutes before teisho. Bhodin Roshi entered the zendo and took his seat on the tan. The lectern was moved up and instead of his katsu he was presented with a back scratcher. In place of his ceramic cup, a gigantic soft drink called a Big Gulp, procured that morning from the local Seven Eleven, was placed before him. The captivating teisho was given, eliciting bursts of laughter. At the end of this teisho, the large *keisu*[2] was struck by the lead chanter to begin recitation of the four Bodhisattva Vows, but when he reached for the small keisu striker, which would have been next, it had mysteriously disappeared. He had no choice but to hit it with his fist, which didn't have the same resonance as the striker and brought some chortles.

At any rate, this is being shared to show that Zen is not allergic to mirth. However, because the teisho from which this chapter was adapted was delivered on the seventh day of sesshin, April Fool's hijinks would not have been appropriate. In each succeeding day of any sesshin, participants are deepening their focus, and quieting and clarifying their minds in the service of reaching a depth in which our true nature is at least glimpsed. Thus, the seventh day of sesshin is the pinnacle of all that cumulative work and it is important not to interrupt that opening to our true nature.

Tibetan Buddhist masters describe that true nature with various terms. One way they speak of our true nature is numinous awareness. Another is luminosity with a quality of cognizance, i.e., wordless understanding. That Mind has existed forever and will never die. We came out of the elixir of beingness. We call it various things in Buddhism but actually any name we try to call it does not really describe it. Bankei Yōtaku, a 17th Century Japanese Buddhist monk, refers to it as "Unborn Mind." Though this Unborn Mind, this numinous awareness has never not been, and no one and nothing is separate from it, humans, whether we realize it or not, are seeking to re-experience it. This yearning has compelled people in many different directions in our lives, some distinctly unhealthy such as addictions, others middling, and still others positive.

---

[2] The very large, bronze, bowl-shaped instrument struck during chants.

BENEFITS OF BEING HONED BY LIFE AND ZEN PRACTICE

Human beings, particularly as we become conditioned, seek innate perfection in hopes of escaping a background sense of incompletion, not realizing we are already complete. So, we start searching for that completion. People search in many different ways hoping always to find permanent happiness. But permanence does not exist. This can engender anxiety since people so often take permanence as a place of safety. And in order to search for that safety, particularly if we've had any negative experiences in our lives, we tend to search outwardly.

Yongey Mingyur Rinpoche learned early in his life to drop the illusion of control. Despite being born into a family of enlightened beings and having had an idyllic childhood, Mingyur Rinpoche was plagued by panic attacks. These panic attacks lasted into his first three-year, three-month, three-day Tibetan retreat. At age 13, fed up with the frequent panic attacks, he returned to his room, ready to face the panic and do whatever was necessary to let go of it before he rejoined the others on the retreat. At last willing to do whatever was necessary, even if painful or frightening, he had reached the essential point at which change can begin to take place. Living life, we unwittingly become content with our suffering even as we complain about it. It's not until we get truly tired of continuing that way that change can happen.

Mingyur Rinpoche chose to make such change by walking right into the terrifying feeling of panic, deeply experiencing the felt-sense and persisting in that practice until the panic attacks were no more. It took three days of his self-imposed solitary confinement until that happened, but afterwards he never had a panic attack again. He had discovered the secret of allowing himself full awareness of the felt-sense of the panic as taught by the 14th Century Tibetan Buddhist master Longchenpa.[3]

Later, after several decades of living in the protected environment of a monastery and teaching his own students, Mingyur Rinpoche sought to test and deepen the level of his awakening by diving right into the world of contemporary India as a wandering pilgrim. For five initially quite challenging years, he removed his Buddhist

---

3 In the book, *You are the Eyes of the World*, (translated by Kennard Lipman and Merrill Peterson, Snow Lion Publications, 2000) you can find a translation of Longchenpa's teachings on how to work with difficult mind states and emotions.

robes and donned the anonymous clothing of a wandering pilgrim, daring to step out of his long-reinforced identity. This is an important precedent for anyone seeking to drop their conditioned identity—not to change your clothes or go on a pilgrimage, necessarily, but to metaphorically do so by letting go your self-identity in the service of realizing who and what you really are.

Once he left the safety of his monastery in India, Mingyur Rinpoche had to struggle with daring to enter the world outside his monastery walls, with which he had always been unfamiliar and from which he had always been protected. Attendants had always done everything for him such as buying first class train tickets, ordering food for him in restaurants, and so on. But committed to an intention to challenge his level of practice by leaving that protected environment, he dared to drop into the unknown without the benefit of any assumed protection he formerly had. This is something that all of us are called to do as we sit in the zendo on our zafu. We all come to zazen with a self-identity of being Somebody, but in order to realize who and what we really are we need to let go that familiar Somebody. To do so, though we don't need to become a wandering pilgrim in India, we are called upon to let go our long-conditioned self-identity. This is a prerequisite to opening to the Truth and realizing the innate freedom we have in being "nobody," yet fully able to function wisely and compassionately in the world.

During his five years of wandering he had many experiences. A most significant experience was in walking right into his awareness that he was dying when severely dehydrated and mortally ill with dysentery. He chose not to avoid going into the sensations of dying. He willingly explored all the sensations in the process of letting go, including the sadness at the thought of not seeing his mother again. He woke up two days later in a hospital after someone had recognized his condition and taken him there, paid for his hospital treatment and left him with some cash to buy food and transportation for a while to recover. The letting go that he had sought had been accomplished. This is one very significant example of being truly honed by life circumstances.[4]

---

[4] You can read Mingyur Rinpoche's incredibly inspiring story of that pilgrimage in his book *In Love with the World: A Monk's Travels Through the Bardos of Living and Dying*.

Most of us reading this have a relatively comfortable lifestyle compared and yet we still hunger for some level of freedom. We have a lot of exterior freedom. Most of us have a certain amount of money or support that allow us to move about in directions we want. But as far as interior freedom, that's what brought us here, a sense of lack of it. And that is the ache in everyone's being until we have found it. We fill that ache with all kinds of things, with travel, with interactions with people, with chasing food, or chasing drink, or chasing drugs, or chasing relationships, or chasing entertainment, or chasing status. There are vast and plentiful ways in which to avoid that inner ache. But sooner or later that ache breaks through and we find ourselves caught in it again.

While most of us are not going to have the opportunity to die of dysentery in India, we all experience more mundane examples of being honed by life. This happens with the pressure of needing to make grades when you're floundering in a school subject. It happens when our teenage romances end with a partner leaving. Bullying is universal in work environments and in family dynamics. Whether or not we get that job promotion impacts our sense of self-worth. At some point a parent or grandparent will die. There are even more intense examples. My granddaughter lost her best friend to suicide when they were sophomores in high school. That year another student at the same school killed himself. My best friend Martha came to Zen at the Rochester Zen Center in the 1980s when her younger son committed suicide. His sister found him dead with the gun in his lap.

Families break up, accidents happen, our loved ones are sent off to war. I have a friend who fell while rock climbing at the age of 21 and has been paraplegic ever since, yet still manages to live an active life now in his 70s. Since the advent of social media there has been an epidemic of loneliness. For teenage girls in particular, social media has resulted in body-shaming and depression severe enough that it has led to suicides. During the COVID-19 pandemic, many families lost multiple family members to an excruciating death. It was so traumatic for doctors and nurses that many had to leave their professions. There are some people who will dodge the bullets for at least most of their life, but then comes the end of life and the fear that accompanies that for so many people.

These are all examples of common suffering in this world today. Yet it is possible to become truly free of the anguish. Psychotherapy can help speed up the process up to a point and is essential for anyone who has experienced trauma. But beyond psychotherapy, sincere, committed, deep Zen practice offers an authentic path to freedom from suffering. Many of us have had untoward experiences getting here. That's actually something that you will begin to realize as a gift if you deepen your practice sufficiently, because it makes us far more empathic to other people who've suffered in one way or another and if we go deeply enough it brings forth a yearning to help relieve suffering in whatever way we can. That is the Bodhisattva Vow. Dissociation is not part of that path. Rather attention and awareness are crucial. But to reach true freedom, there has to be commitment, persistence, and a willingness to stay in for the long haul with an authentic teacher.

Chapter Nine
A Story of Transformation: ACES and Zen

WE LIVE IN what is known in Buddhism as the *saha* world or the world of samsara—a world characterized by dukkha. Although dukkha is often translated as "suffering," it spans a range of mind states from boredom to agony and everything in between. As this is being written, there are brutal wars going on in several parts of the world. Here in America a recent video taken during an hour in one of the cars of a New York City subway train traveling its route was posted to a news outlet. During that hour in which the video was filmed there were multiple fights, gunshots and people injured. Everyday, millions of people ride the subways for work, shopping, and recreation in New York City. Dukkha, whether in the form of boredom or extreme violence, isn't something that happens only "over there" to "other people."

Exposure to these events and even the news of these events conditions us. That conditioning limits our view of the world and our abilities within it. Our conditioning begins even before birth as our developing brains experience the environment. Within our mother's womb we are able to sense her levels of joy or stress. After we're born, we continue that development and continue that exposure to conditioning. How that early childhood develops for each one of us results in what are considered four types of attachment styles depending on how the relationship with our primary caregivers unfold. The term "attachment styles" refers to how we relate to people and things in our lives, particularly significant people.

If we've had a mainly happy, supportive, safe, and caring environment in our earlier years, through those experiences we are conditioned to assume a world of relative friendliness and safety. If our main interactions with our primary caregivers have been mixed, sometimes supportive, sometimes not, we become conditioned to assume the world is not trustworthy and not necessarily safe. We won't go into a description of all four attachment styles, but you get the gist of it; our earlier experiences of life result in a view of our environment and the world as having qualities that mimic the experiences we had with our primary caregivers in our earlier days.

These experiences combine to develop an internal story of who we assume we are, which results in what can be termed a "self-image." This self-image tends to drive our outlook on life and our behaviors in response to it. If we've been treated as if we don't matter, for example, then our assumption grows that we really don't matter and that story, which creates the self-image of somebody that doesn't matter, will drive our compensatory behavior in dysfunctional ways. With this self-image, there's often an underlying rage as well, and through it we may project a self-image onto others and treat them as if they don't matter, without even realizing we're doing so, and being surprised at the other person's reaction.

Then there is an ongoing human draw to try to change the outcome of things. We've had a bad experience so we're often drawn back to that experience. We tend to go back into situations where it didn't work out in an attempt to fix it so it does work out. Part of this too is a mindset that this is what we deserve. It calibrates our expectations for the world which then creates our experience in the world. The specifics of our self-image significantly circumscribe the world we experience. Yet, we are so much more than this "story."

Doctor Vincent Filetti in 1985 was chief of Kaiser Permanente's Department of Preventive Medicine in San Diego where a program was developed in their obesity clinic that was initially highly effective in helping people drop significant weight. As the program unfolded, something mysterious happened, obese people were able to lose a significant amount of weight and then suddenly began gaining the weight back again and dropping out of the program. Investigating this phenomenon led Dr. Filetti to change course and conduct decades more research that uncovered why this continued to happen in a high proportion of his obesity patients. In the late 1990s this extensive research delivered a list of what were termed adverse childhood experiences (ACEs).

It seems these ACEs lead to significant behavior patterns such as overeating or other self-destructive behaviors as we attempt to protect ourselves from further adverse experiences. What are these ACEs? "Adverse childhood experiences (ACEs) are defined as preventable, potentially traumatic events that occur among persons aged <18 years and are associated with numerous negative outcomes."[1] Data shows that not only in the United States but throughout the world ACEs are widely experienced. There is a list of eight ACEs that include the following:

- Physical, sexual, and emotional abuse
- Emotional and physical neglect
- Living with a family member with mental health or substance use disorders
- Witnessing domestic violence
- Sudden separation from a loved one
- Poverty
- Racism and discrimination
- Violence in the community

As we read this list we can reflect on our own history. Growing up offers us many experiences of these challenges and the opportunity to learn how to respond to them effectively or alternatively cause us to dig deeper into our protective modes of behavior. The DSM-5-TR—the most recent edition of the Diagnostic and Statistical Manual of Mental Disorders—is a thick book describing conditions such as bipolar disorder or schizophrenia, along with a wide range of dysfunctional behavior patterns people can develop in response to life experience. It's well known, for example, that a high proportion of people diagnosed with borderline personality disorder (BPD) had experienced sexual abuse as children. Common characteristics of BPD can include, among other behaviors, self-harming and risky behavior, both of which could be understood as a cry for help. These compensatory patterns interfere with our free experience of life as we seek to feel safe, to feel loved, and to feel worthy. If we could only realize that we already are worthy of respect, honor, and love even if our behavior does not reflect that.

---

1 From the Center for Disease Control's website, https://www.cdc.gov/.

It's important to recognize that the development of self-protective behaviors in response to ACEs happens on a spectrum. Adverse experiences do not automatically mean a diagnosis of BPD. That is just one example, and a rather extreme example, of self-protective behavior that can occur. Some of these behaviors resulting from ACEs can be quite subtle. Pre-test anxiety, reticence about going to a new place or meeting new people, these are a couple of the more subtle examples of behaviors we adopt to protect ourselves from pain.

Yet at the same time there's often a sense of something freer barely out of reach. And that sense is accurate. Since time immemorial, people have experienced that freedom. If we are fortunate, we eschew non-productive ways of seeking it such as alcoholism, rage, addiction, and turn instead to spiritual practice. Rinzai Zen offers an authentic means to gradually see where we are caught in dysfunction. With continuing motivation and commitment, using these means, we can gradually drop these dysfunctional behaviors and increasingly open to that innate freedom that is revealed through this committed practice.

Metta meditation, also known as loving kindness, is one of the effective practices in working with the results of ACEs. Recognize, however, that children undergoing ACEs generally conclude that these bad things are happening to them because they're not good enough. For that reason, becoming able to effectively do the loving kindness meditation can be a challenge. It can take us several years before we can offer ourselves intentions of loving kindness without resistance. In other words, the positive feelings about ourselves and others that are a product of regular loving kindness practice has brought about a subtle change in our self-image. This practice and the practice of susok'kan are usually a challenge as well because we are practiced in avoiding feeling uncomfortable feelings; but with the help of effective psychotherapy, the example of fellow sangha members, and an authentic Zen teacher, if we persist we will gradually become more open and more free.

In the 1980s, a lovely woman came frequently to sittings at the Rochester Zen Center where I was in residential training at the time. You could see the brightness in her but you could also feel the intense anxiety for approval and connection. It was uncomfortable for many people to be in her presence because of this apparent neediness that was prominent in any encounter with her. As I got to know her over the years, I could also feel a great courage resonant in her and a determination to become free although she had no idea what she needed to become free from. She continued to persist in her practice while also leading a full professional life.

As the years went by and more of her story became known to her, in addition to continuing her zazen and increasing it with attending many sesshin, she began working with an experienced therapist, focusing on pre-verbal trauma. With therapy and deepening Zen practice, the horrors of her childhood and adolescence began to have less power over her. And today, decades later, one no longer feels that anxious neediness for love and approval. Her life has changed radically. Drawn to her compassion and wisdom, people now seek to be in her presence. Her life is rich and deeply fulfilling as she continues to deepen her Zen practice significantly and work effectively with her history. Today she is so radically different, so joyful to be around, so caring and open, quite different from how she was when I first met her. Here is an example of the ongoing power of persistent Zen practice coupled with appropriate psychotherapy. While not every one of us has experienced the ongoing trauma that this woman had, the potential for all of us is to reach a point where we freely live our innate wisdom and compassion—our innate perfection.

It takes time to accomplish this. It's not instantaneous. But with dogged persistence and willingness to walk into where it hurts with the help of effective practice, especially the susok'kan, a regular *metta* (loving kindness) practice and the guidance of an authentic teacher I have no doubt that you can accomplish this.[2]

---

2   There are recordings of loving kindness metta meditations on Mountain Gate's website https://www.sanmonjizen.org/teishos.html#.html

Chapter Ten
Struggle and Transformation in Spiritual Practice

ZEN PRACTICE IS UNIQUE. It is unlike anything else most people have done in their lives. Fundamental to the practice is being tossed out of our usual way of experiencing through the lens of our self-image and thus our behavior patterns. Because of the vulnerability and trust required in working effectively with a Zen teacher it is vital to choose a spiritual group and/or teacher with discernment. As Roshi Kapleau used to say, "it's like marriage: before marriage keep both eyes open, after marriage keep one eye open." The American Zen Teachers Association (AZTA) lists teachers who have gone through significant training and whose teaching venue must have an ethics policy including a specific means through which members of the group who feel they have been treated unethically can appeal to a neutral group to investigate the purported event and take action as needed.[1]

Our accustomed way of functioning, and we're well trained in this, is to use words and calculations to research answers to questions and navigate daily challenges. Through these means we search for comfort. In that case, why are we drawn to Zen? We come to Zen practice normally with a question but it's rarely a question in words. It's a sense, a background feeling that there's something more, something beyond our ordinary focus in our usual way of living. In order to do Zen practice, we have to step out of our customary mode of experiencing.

Mario Montese, whose story you read in an earlier chapter, says as the spiritual teacher he is now, "I take your questions away." Centuries earlier, a Chinese Chan master Rinzai Gigen—or Linji Yixuan as he's called in Chinese—said the same thing in different words. His teachings are recorded in the *Record of Rinzai* (*Rinzai Roku*):

---

[1] https://zenteachers.org/members-of-azta.

> Among all the students from every quarter who are followers of the Way, none has yet come before me without being dependent on something. Here I hit them right from the start. If they come forth using their hands, I hit them on the hands; if they come forth using their mouths, I hit them on the mouth; if they come forth using their eyes, I hit them on the eyes.[2] Not one has yet come before me in solitary freedom. All are clambering after the worthless contrivances of the men of old. As for myself, I haven't a single dharma to give to people.[3]

Normally filled with assumptions and questions, we begin Zen by dragging our ideas into our encounters with practice and a teacher. But as Mario and Rinzai both point out, in order to reach that promise of boundless freedom offered by the practice, we need to let go of the comfort afforded by those expectations about what life is because that vast freedom cannot be found through words. Thus in our earlier years of Zen practice it can be quite unsettling as our normal ways of navigating through life are useless here. We enter the sanzen room and demonstrate before our teacher who rings us out saying, "keep working, keep working…" leaving us still befuddled.

These earlier years of work (and, yes, it can take years) are often described as feeling like a blind man whose staff is taken from him, is turned around three times, pushed to the ground and told to find his way home. Hakuin Zenji, centuries ago, painted his version of this in a well-known piece entitled, "Blind Men Crossing a Bridge."[4]

We all have our comfort zones even if they are uncomfortable. And, yes, even a life of pain and suffering can serve some psychological purpose in being comforting. We human beings so often fear change and as a result we seek permanence. Everything does

---

2   Of course this "hitting" is metaphorical. Because Rinzai's statement here is also a koan in the Rinzai sect, we'll not go into further comments about it as the value of koans is lost if there's too much explanation.

3   *The Record of Linji*, Translation and commentary by Ruth Fuller Sasaki, edited by Thomas Yūhō Kirchner, Pg. 22.

4   By googling "Hakuin's painting Blind Men Crossing a Bridge" you can find images of this work online.

change, however. There is no permanence. As a pertinent example of the hold this fear of change has on people, when Flora Courtois, at an important stage in her own search for a Truth that was always true, had a vision in which she was part of a cave-dwelling family in ancient times. The family decided to venture to the opening of the cave. She was amazed by the vast plane of light and expansive view, but to her dismay the rest of the family turned around and went back inside. That openness, that freedom, was too frightening for them. This expresses in metaphor how it is for us entering Zen practice. As we get close to the precipice mentioned in earlier chapters, it's a very challenging time in our Zen practice. But if we are willing to persist and endure the discomfort and walk into the fear, we will discover what we had always been searching for. The result is an experience of immense freedom that unfolds more and more deeply as we persist. As you've heard before, the work of the long maturation is vital if we are to continue to experience that liberation and live it.

There is a lot of work that needs to be done by everyone to reach this point of deep freedom. If that sounds daunting, not to worry; it's not grim the whole way through. The work becomes fulfilling as it rewards us with increasing moments of insight. In the words of one Zen student,

> Feelings of loneliness and not belonging have been persistent throughout my life. During residential Zen practice at Mountain Gate, which is to say many sesshin, as well as regularly meeting with a trauma-therapist (who happened to spend twenty years of his life as a Zen monk), I began to see through those feelings of loneliness. I learned that my "loner narrative" was actually serving a function in my life. It was trying to protect and keep me feeling safe and comfortable by myself since groups of people seemed inherently threatening, which I felt for good reason. Not to mention, this narrative has made me feel somehow special in the world—a sort of wandering poet type not so different from celebrated literary figures like Jack Kerouac or Ernest

Hemingway. "The world doesn't understand me!" these figures cry out not realizing just how much ego there is in a statement like that.

Seeing this pattern of loneliness, I began to have opportunities to test and challenge it and find out that I am not an innately lonesome or solitary person. I experienced a breakthrough while getting involved with an art gallery in Northern New Mexico. I made some art for the gallery, began attending events, and got acquainted with other artists, which, although positive, created a lot of social-anxiety and inner-tension for me.

For example, I volunteered to help out at one of the gallery's fundraising events. With several DJs, loud electronic dance music, and a crowded room, the event became overwhelming for me. I found myself receding into my loner narrative. I felt as though I were a shy twenty-year-old college student again, wallflowering at a party, desperate for genuine connection but painfully quiet and unsure of how to fit in. Feelings of loneliness and exclusion took over, including a long story about how I'll never fit in, or be accepted, and who cares if I'm not accepted anyway, and maybe I'm just in the wrong place, and there's a better life somewhere else, and etc. and etc.

That night I slept at a friend's house—somehow ignoring the fact that this friend was fully accepting of me, appreciative of my presence, and happy to have me in his home. The next morning my loner narrative continued as I strolled through the Taos Plaza sighing to myself in the cold, gray rain—very dramatic indeed. I was about to get in my car and drive, still sighing, back to Mountain Gate. But there was more awareness of the loner narrative I'd been developing, and I wondered, "Why am I so lonely right now?" I was no longer asking that as an external question meaning why is the world so cruel to me, but more as an internal question of why am I behaving this way, why is my perspective such that everything seems lonesome. I suddenly realized that I don't have to keep doing this.

The narrative loosened and no longer seemed as real, even if I still felt it. I decided to test the narrative. Instead of immediately driving out of town, I walked over to the art gallery where there's always someone working or painting in the studio. Sure enough, a couple of artist acquaintances were there and we had a beautiful conversation about art, life paths, and relationships. I found myself smiling and enjoying their company and realizing that they enjoyed my company too, that I wasn't some kind of interruption or drag on their day. The husk of loneliness fell off completely during that conversation, I shared a warm hug with one of those new friends before I left, and could feel my brain and body repatterning itself for connection and social enjoyment. Instead of driving back to Mountain Gate feeling sorry for myself, I drove back cheerful and optimistic that I could open to new relationships and new experiences.

It has been a lot of hard work to get to this point of deep change—I behaved one way for almost thirty years and am now behaving in a totally new and more free way. I feel as though I'm losing track of who I am, or who I thought I was, and it turns out that's a really wonderful thing.

Perseverance is essential. All you have to do is keep plowing along one foot after the other and eventually little by little you will begin to experience greater and greater levels of freedom. Sometimes people are afraid of freedom. If we're free, how on Earth are we going to know what to do or how to act? What's going to guide us in life? If we're truly free, if we have truly let go, then there is a deeper awareness that comes forth or is revealed. Yes, there will be a new way of living—a new way of living guided by a clear, ongoing sense of what to do in each moment. At first there will be intrusions of habit patterns of greed, anger, and delusion from which we have temporarily freed ourselves. But if our awakening is deep enough, it's as if there's an inner guide to appropriate behavior. It's always there, it's just covered up by our conditioning. We instinctively sense where to move next, what to do next, how to speak next, and it's not driven by ideas. It's a natural flow with the process of being. And it's always right; in my experience it's always right.

昭

Chapter Eleven
Luminous Transparency
and the Rapids of Life

Things change; they're always changing and they will continue to change forever. Metaphorically, as we flow through the experience of living, there will sometimes be smooth waters and there will be rapids of greater or lesser intensity, and sometimes cataclysmic waterfalls. For most human beings, change can be unsettling and we attempt to establish some level of stability in our lives in order to feel safe. The death toll for the massive 2023 earthquake that impacted eastern Turkey and Syria exceeded 60,000 people. The people living in that area of Syria were unsupported by the government and left desperate for aid. Decades before that, the death toll from an even more massive earthquake in Kobe, Japan, which was further impacted when gas pipes broke causing fire to race through whole neighborhoods, brought yet more destruction. These are examples of life's cataclysmic waterfalls, and yet there is something beneath the turmoil.

As that catastrophic day in Kobe in 1995 drew to an end, an elderly woman stood on a pile of rubble gazing at the setting sun with a look of profound peace on her face. She had opened to that something deeper. We all have that something. It's our true mind. It's not outside of us. This is our face before our parents were born and what any number of other koans point to. It doesn't make sense in normal logic and yet it is absolutely, phenomenally true. Even in the midst of devastation there is this profound peace, this profound okayness, this profound courage that knows no bounds, that allows us to meet adversity without being caught by it.

Kalu Rinpoche, who died in 1989, was a renowned teacher in the Tibetan Buddhist Karma Kagyu lineage. Tibetan Buddhist teachers seem to have a gift for expressing the dharma in easily accessible ways. So it was that whenever Kalu Rinpoche would come through Santa Fe to teach his students there, we Zen folks would attend his public talks. In a book of his teachings, *Luminous Mind: The Way of the Buddha*,[1] at the head of each chapter is a quote from another Tibetan master. The chapter, "One Mind, Two States," begins with a quote by the Third Karmapa "As long as mind is not recognized, the wheel of existence turns. When this is understood, the state of Buddha is nothing other than that. There is nothing that can be described as either existing or not existing. May the nature of reality, the true nature of the Buddha mind be recognized." This is what the *Heart of Perfect Wisdom* (the *Prajna Paramita Hridaya*), a core teaching of the Buddha, also expresses. In Kalu Rinpoche's words, "Mind has two faces, two facets, which are two aspects of one reality. These are enlightenment and illusion."

When Bodhidharma was young, a visitor came and taught the *Prajna Paramita*,

> The Bodhisattva of Compassion from the depths of prajna wisdom saw the emptiness of all five skandhas[2] and sundered the bonds that create suffering. Know then form here is only emptiness, emptiness only form. Form is no other than emptiness. Emptiness no other than form. Feeling, thought, and choice, consciousness itself are the same as this. Dharmas (phenomena) here are empty, all are the primal void. None are born or die, nor are they stained or pure, nor do they wax or wane. So in emptiness no form, no feeling, thought or choice, nor is there consciousness. No eye, ear, nose, tongue, body-mind, no color, sound, smell, taste, touch, or what the mind takes hold of...

On hearing this, the young boy pointed to his nose and said, "But I have a nose! I have eyes," and it became his koan.[3] How can a core teaching of the Buddha speak of no eyes, no ears, but we can look in

---

1 *Luminous Mind: The Way of the Buddha*, Kalu Rinpoche, Wisdom Publications, 1997, pg. 19.

2 The components of one's being that begets clinging—eye, ear, nose, tongue, body, and mind. It has also been translated as form, sensations, perceptions, mental formations, and discernment.

3 In my own beginning Zen practice, although I was assigned the koan Mu, what really grabbed me were the questions: how could form be empty and how could emptiness have form?

the mirror and of course see these physical features.

It cannot be more emphasized: true reality is that form is emptiness and emptiness is form. This does not deny that we have a physical form, experiences, desires, etc. To experience this Truth at the deepest level, i.e., far removed from intellectual analysis, is profoundly liberating. Through committed Zen practice it can be uncovered. The process of uncovering it is what makes Zen practice so challenging. This cover that blinds our eyes to true reality has developed as a result of our conditioning and so we have an investment in it. In an attempt to block out awareness of painful and traumatic experiences we've had, that cover is as protective as a pearl is around a grain of sand that would otherwise agitate an oyster. Hence, to reach that profound understanding and the liberation it affords, it's necessary to open Pandora's box and work deeply with everything that flies out. Because what is stored in that box is the product of our painful experiences, it can help speed up the process of working with what comes out of the box if we not only do Zen practice but also work with a psychotherapist familiar with Zen practice.

It's important to recognize that Pandora's box may be full of challenging experiences. Awareness of them all is rarely simultaneous as our mind is, generally, self-protective. Things will come up when they're ready to come up. They seem to have their own timeline. Sometimes we may become aware there's an unidentified something lurking in the background that is uncomfortable and calling for attention. With intention and patience, the time will come when it reveals itself. This can take a long time. Again, increasing your Zen practice and working with a therapist will allow it to become conscious sooner. To quote the Third Karmapa again, "As long as mind is not recognized, the wheel of existence turns." It is through the process of dismantling this self-created protective cover that truth begins to be revealed. As this process continues, we find ourselves both with moments of greater intensity but also moments of greater peace and ease. To continue, "There is nothing that can be described as either existing or not existing. May the nature of reality, the true nature of the Buddha mind be recognized." And that's what we're working towards doing here at Mountain Gate. We have the tools: susok'kan and the koans. All we need is the determination, the guidance, the willingness to go through whatever we have to go through to uncover that luminous transparency and experience the true, ongoing liberation that results.

So here Kalu Rinpoche continues, "Mind has two faces, two facets, which are two aspects of one reality. These are enlightenment and illusion." And the conditioning begets illusion. Conditioning is an essential part of being a human being because without it we would, for example, walk into fire undeterred and we would do other dangerous things that would shorten our life. So, there is conditioning, but within conditioning there can be extremity. As an example, I went to high school in a very small town in Northern Indiana that was about 50 miles away from Chicago and we would sometimes go into Chicago on the weekends to the Museum of Science and Industry. Michigan Avenue in those days was a very upscale avenue of expensive stores, but if you went two blocks south you were in danger of getting mugged in plain daylight. You can choose to walk down Michigan Avenue or you can choose to go two blocks away and wander in the not-so-great district taking the risk that something untoward will happen. There are certain decisions that we can make in our life that will make a difference; some of them are out of our hands of course, but some of them like coming to Zen practice and sticking with it will eventually bring about a positive result. Others, like wandering into traffic assuming you're invincible, will not. We have a certain amount of choice in these matters.

But what is this illusion that is the flip side of enlightenment? It begins with the creation of a self-image as the result of our experiences. An event happens in our life, and because of our perception of that event, a set of expectations is created and skews our perception of future events.

There is a classic example of a police report of an accident in which a car runs a red light and t-bones another car passing through the intersection. As the police ask each of the people witnessing the accident, they each come up with differing and sometimes opposing memories of what happened. It happens so suddenly we don't have time to think about it and so we experience it from a place of mind that is totally one with the experience. But when the police interrogate the witnesses about what happened, they each have a different version of what they saw.

When I was in high school, I was at a neighbor's house, outside in the yard facing the highway and watched a car coming along with a person on a bicycle riding parallel to the car as they approached a side street. Suddenly the bicyclist turned and rode right in front of the car. The driver of the car in an effort to avoid the bicycle rider whipped the steering wheel and the car fell over on its side, successfully missing the bicycle and its rider who continued on unaware of what they had caused. Witnessing that accident, initially I was speechless. I could not tell my friend, whose back was to the accident, what I had just seen. In the shock of the experience, all I could do was point. Direct experiences like this are witnessed without a filter prior to the next stage of perception which is to analyze it and create a story from that initial, raw experience. This makes it possible to speak of it.

Some time ago at the Rochester Zen Center we had ended an evening sitting and Roshi Kapleau and the rest of the sangha were out in the Link Building chatting. One person had just seen the movie *Crouching Tiger, Hidden Dragon* and was describing it to the roshi. "It was violent," he said, "but it was a great movie." Roshi's response was, "You need to be careful about what you're putting into your head." The Buddha said something like this millennia ago when he urged his students to be with like-minded people who are also drawn to zazen for the purpose of freeing themselves from painful behavior patterns. What we expose ourselves to, influences our behavior.

Years ago, there was a multi-year psychological study following eight-, nine-, and ten-year-old kids into young adulthood. During those years, the kids were playing violent video games on a regular basis. The study showed a link between playing violent video games and violent actions as they grew older. The violence that they had witnessed and played with in those videogames had influenced their behavior. It's harder to come to awakening if your mind is filled with negativity and violence. Doing metta (loving kindness) meditation can positively affect our experience of being, just as addiction to violent video games, movies, TV shows, or music can also affect our mind in the direction of violence.

Yet that luminous transparency is always there beneath it all. We can open to that. It's an alive state of mind. It's not la la land. It's real. It's freedom from the conditioning. It's freedom from the stance of being a victim, for example, or having a history, or needing to be a certain way. It's freedom to be who you really are, which is perfect, whole, and complete just as you are. And when we can realize that, of course then we have to work on what's called the long maturation, which is to bring our life into line with what we've realized because habit patterns will persist, and that's some of the strong work of practice. But the first work is to work with our conditioning, with the ways we feel stuck, the ways we feel helpless, the ways we feel like we can't do it, the ways we feel like this is impossible to do. How can we open to something that we can't even describe and yet countless human beings have done so for more than 2500 years and achieved that immense freedom that comes from not being caught in your conditioning? You can do it too; it just takes time, work, commitment, and some help from a guide.

Chapter Twelve
Nirvana

MARK EPSTEIN has been a practicing psychiatrist as well as a Theravadin Buddhist practitioner for many decades. He has written a number of excellent books expressing his insights into meditation practice informed by his understanding of psychiatry. One of those books in particular, *Going on Being: Life at the Crossroads of Buddhism and Psychotherapy* is especially relevant in this chapter. His background and experience make him a perfect person to speak of these. In the traditional Japanese Zen way of teaching, because of the nature of Japanese culture to this day, psychotherapy has not played a significant role. But American culture is quite different and in my experience there's a wide area of overlap between therapy and Zen practice. While therapy can help a person work with their dysfunctional behaviors with the aim of achieving a certain level of ease in their life, utilizing both Zen and therapy can take a person far deeper, all the way to true liberation.

In the context of psychotherapy, we can learn to more effectively navigate the strictures caused by our investment in a self-image, while Zen practice goes beyond that to help us see through and dissolve our attachment to a self-image, rendering us totally free of its control over our lives. Yet, Zen practice without therapy can be too narrow for many people. Historically, when people have done Zen practice and not done therapy to address their psychological issues, things did not always turn out well. There are unfortunate examples of this in the cases of Buddhist "teachers" who sexually abused their students. When Harada Roshi was asked how this could possibly happen by someone who is authorized to teach Zen, his response was, "They didn't spend a long enough time in the monastery." Traditional Zen practice has been likened to diving into a deep pool and going straight to the bottom focused on achieving awakening and bypassing the psychological debris we have accumulated and may still be accumulating in our lives. In contrast, the long maturation, which can begin even before you sit on the cushion for the first time and is a vital part of practice, can naturally involve psychotherapy. Committing to the process of the long maturation, along with our deepening Zen practice, may slow our dive to the bottom of that pool as we clean out the psychological debris along the way, but will result in a far more broad and deep awakening.

The difference is that with the combination of therapy and Zen we learn to navigate our lives and conditioning with more skill and therefore more ease, as we go much farther than that to become increasingly free of psychological "velcro." As you know, velcro is a two-part material for attaching things. There is the fuzzy side and the side with tiny hooks and when you put the two parts together, they stick to each other. To continue the metaphor, we are upholstered in either the fuzzy part or the hooked part. For example, you're in an office setting and there are some of your co-workers and higher ups with whom you feel a harmonious connection. Metaphorically, if you're upholstered in the fuzzy side, coming into contact with people or things also upholstered in the fuzzy side there will be nothing to get hooked by. But that irritating person in the office is upholstered in the hook side; otherwise you wouldn't be so irritated by them. It doesn't matter which type of velcro we're upholstered in; it's coming into contact with the opposite side that will catch us. Going to therapy can help us learn how to navigate our velcro so we can more skillfully manage difficult situations. Whereas Zen practice offers the possibility of gradually removing our velcro so that no matter what velcro we come in contact with it won't catch us. We will be clear and free of that conditioning so that we will be able to work with difficult situations with perfect ease since we won't be attached to a specific outcome.

That said, what is this freedom? In his book Epstein writes: "Nirvana is a Buddha's word for freedom, not for death." People commonly assume that nirvana means death or even "the good death." But, in reality, it means the end of suffering as a result of no longer being caught in attachments; in other words, total liberation. The fear of what we assume death means is what is behind a lot of anxiety in Zen practice. The anxiety is also fueled by the assumption that we will no longer exist if we go too far into our practice. In one sense, who we think we are will little by little disappear and who we really are, which is not a self-image resulting from conditioning, will be seen through as the false image it actually is.

But before that there is a struggle with yearning for that freedom and being terrified of it. In his poem, "The Fall of Hyperion," John Keats, who was battling tuberculosis at the time, describes the tension in this moment between fear and potential freedom. He writes of a vision in which he is presented with a set of heavenly stairs and confronted with a great fear of death. The metaphor in Zen practice for those stairs is the edge of the cliff. A spirit compels him to either climb the stairs or simply die unfreed where he was at the bottom of the steps:

> "If thou canst not ascend
> These steps, die on that marble where thou art.
> Thy flesh near cousin to the common dust
> Will parch for lack of nutriment thy bones
> Will whither in few years, and vanish so
> That not the quickest eye could find a grain
> Of what thou now art on that pavement cold.
> The sands of thy short life are spent this hour
> And no hand in the universe can turn
> Thy hourglass."

In response, Keats finds himself caught between the terror and yearning for liberation:

> I... felt the tyranny
> Of that fierce threat and hard task proposed.
> Prodigious seem'd the toil, the leaves were yet
> Burning when suddenly a palsied chill
> Struck from the paved level up my limbs
> And was ascending quick to put cold grasp
> Upon those streams that pulse beside the throat:
> I shriek'd; and the sharp anguish of my shriek
> Stung my own ears I strove hard to escape

> The numbness; strove to gain the lowest step.
> Slow, heavy, deadly was my pace: the cold
> Grew stifling, suffocating, at the heart;
> And when I clasp'd my hands I felt them not.
> One minute before death, my iced foot touch'd
> The lowest stair; and as it touch'd, life seem'd
> To pour in at the toes: I mounted up.

In these powerful lines, Keats chooses, not without inner conflict and immense difficulty, to step into the challenge, to step into his fear. It is by walking into this fear that he then opens to life. As was said in a previous chapter, a fear of death is a fear of life, and to drop that fear is to truly live. The spirit then explains Keats' experience to him:

> "Thou hast felt
> What 'tis to die and live again before
> Thy fated hour. That thou hast power to do so
> Is thy own safety; thou hast dated on
> Thy doom." "High Prophetess," said I, "purge off,
> Benign, if so it please thee, my mind's film."
> "None can usurp this height," return'd that shade.[1]

The spirit assures Keats that he has walked through his fear of death and purged his "mind's film" or self-image and that no one can take away his freedom. Keats died of tuberculosis before completing this poem. It was published posthumously in 1856.

As Shidō Bunan, Zen grandfather of the great master Hakuin, said, "If you die before you die, you won't die when you die." As you get closer and closer to coming to an insight or even a kensho then fear naturally can arise. It really is a fear of disappearing, a fear of death, and it is important to make friends with that, to embrace it with open arms. Feel the bodily sensations that express that fear. This can require repeated efforts as initially we will still fear those sensations. But continue to sense more deeply into them and eventually they will dissipate. We can plateau in the middle of this process

---

[1] "The Fall of Hyperion," John Keats, 1856, public domain.

and not reach that state of mind where fear and anxiety no longer have any hold on us. To keep that from happening, as we go into the bodily sensations, the sense of energy that expresses that anxiety or fear, it's important to explore the sensations, not just to sit there with them. Rather, utilize an openness to possibility, a not-knowing for sure what it actually feels like or what it is actually like and discerning the ever more subtle sensations.

This is important because eventually we won't have a choice; ultimately everything will be taken away. We can't take anything with us, despite what many cultures have assumed. Items expected to be "needed" or beneficial to the deceased in the next life are often buried in tombs and graves with bodies or burnt with them in cremation ovens. There's a vast buried army of life-size statues of horses and warriors in Xi'an, China. It was believed that the important person buried in this tomb would be continuing on to a next corporeal life in which he would benefit from having that army at his disposal. In present-day Chinese culture, when a person is cremated, various paper representations of automobiles, houses, money, and other possessions are included in that cremation. Contemporary major religions teach that the person we think we are will continue on into heaven, hell, or purgatory depending on how much they have sinned. Some people are so terrified by the fear of becoming no more that they go to great expense to have their bodies cryogenically frozen and therefore preserved in the assumption that they will slip back into that same body and continue life as before. These assumptions are driven by a need to posit a continuing life after death. But what is death really?

There is that great fear of dying and that is endemic in people because we don't know what it will be like. It's a fear of change, of the unknown. The hope in burying presumably-needed objects for the next life after we die is an attempt to convince ourselves that there's a concrete future. Buddhism teaches that life is eternal, that what we call death and what we call birth are nothing but the emergence and the return to the sea of potentiality, the sea of eternal life from which we come forth into corporeal form and dissolve back into with our corporeal death.

Socrates was said to be surrounded by his weeping students as the poison that he was condemned to drink began working its way up to his heart. He said to them, "To fear death, gentlemen, is nothing other than to think oneself wise when one is not; for it is to think one knows what one does not know. No man knows whether death may not even turn out to be the greatest of blessings for a human being; and yet people fear it as if they knew for certain that it is the greatest of evils."[2] What is death but change? Dukkha, which is a characteristic of unawakened life, is the fear of ceaseless change. Most people in the West, with the positive exception of many Native American peoples, are uncomfortable with, or even terrified of, change. Yet change is the only certainty in life. This fear of change underlies our fear of coming to awakening, of the experience that is nirvana.

---

[2] *The Wheel of Death: A Collection of Writings from Zen Buddhist and Other Sources on Death—Rebirth—Dying*, edited by Philip Kapleau, Harper & Row Publishers, 1971, since out of print.

Chapter Thirteen
A Featureless Map of Zen Practice

Chapter Thirteen
A Featureless Map of Cell Biology

IN THIS CHAPTER I want to give you something as close as possible to a map of Zen practice, because there are no precise instructions. It's moment-to-moment suggestions and guidance as things come up for people but there is a pattern of how it generally proceeds.

There's something in our life that inspires us to get in touch with some form of spiritual practice. It is not anything we can ordinarily put in words, but it is something that draws us to the practice. After my grandmother gave me a bible for my tenth birthday, I began intensely searching Christianity for some access to that mystery I sensed was beyond words. At the time, I couldn't find it. From my youthful ignorance, I studied the bible intently and even taught Sunday school in my teenage years. But I hadn't recognized how profound the teachings of Jesus were.

Still, this yearning to remerge with that seemingly lost mystery remained. It came more into focus in the early 1970s when Transcendental Meditation (TM) became popular in the United States. I had always felt that I could reconnect with what was real beyond words if I had the right tools. When TM became popular, I thought maybe that was the right tool. I was interested in doing meditation and TM seemed simple and not too intimidating. Although I was living in Turkey at the time, I was back in the United States for a visit. The friend who I was staying with was going through the initial process involving flowers, money, and guru worship that was required before one began a TM practice. When I saw those preliminaries, I lost my interest and instead called up a Tibetan Buddhist group to find out their meditation schedule.

Why Buddhist? I'd already lived for five years in the Buddhist countries of Myanmar and Thailand with my husband who was a Foreign Service Officer employed by the US State Department and posted in those countries. In Myanmar, my husband was the consul in Mandalay and we were invited to many of the typical ceremonies when young boys, six- to eight-years-old, had their heads shaved and put on Buddhist robes to enter the monastery for the first time.[1] When we lived in Chiang Mai, Thailand, the house we rented was brand new and owned by a young Thai man who had recently graduated from university in the United States. Because the house was new it needed to be blessed with a ceremony led by a small group of Buddhist monks. Naturally, our whole family attended that ceremony. As well, our landlord was engaged to be married and typically in the Theravadin tradition, the husband-to-be spends 100 days as a monk in a monastery before the wedding. We had attended both his ordination and, later, his Buddhist wedding. The ceremonies and our times spent around the various temples in Myanmar and Thailand felt comfortable and familiar.

When someone in Turkey told me that he did TM and zazen, I was still wanting to do something quick, easy, and non-threatening, which TM seemed to be—fifteen minutes a day with your eyes closed, relaxed, and repeating a word. What could be threatening about that? Despite my previous hesitation, I said, "Oh good, teach me how to do TM!" He said he couldn't because I'd have to go to New York to get a mantra. Financially, this was not an option. He then offered to teach me zazen. But, interested in a quick fix, I responded, "no, thanks." There was something that seemed frightening about committing to Zen practice. This is probably what kept me from following through with the Tibetan group. Some months later, however, suddenly the rug was pulled out from under my feet and I lost everything that I held dear in my life.

The karma to be married to my wonderful husband vanished. And when the karma for something ends, nothing can be done to reverse that. I was trying to maintain my connection to the marriage, but it was impossible. As this was happening, I was continuing my architecture studies at Middle East Technical University, which was supposed to be an English language university. My physics professor,

---

1 Theravadin Buddhism is practiced in Myanmar and Thailand. In Mahayana Buddhism ordination is considered to be for life, while in the Theravadin tradition one can enrobe and disrobe many times in their life. For example, the consulate driver always took his two weeks of annual vacation to enter the monastery.

who was Turkish, and recognized that everyone in the class was Turkish (except me), decided on the second day to begin teaching in Turkish. This happened only a couple months after I arrived in Turkey and did not know enough of the language to manage a physics course. Then, she rescheduled the class right on top of my architecture history class, which I found truly fascinating since it went farther back in time than any Western history of architecture course did. Further, I was in an advanced math course, this one taught in English by an Egyptian, but I lacked the critical prerequisites for the course and found myself making terrible grades, which was a blow to my sense of self as I'd always been a top-level student. My husband, in his pain, asked for a transfer. At the time they were only transferring Foreign Service Officers to Saigon, and this was near the end of the war in Vietnam. The State Department determined that my sons had to be living with their father if the Department was to pay for their schooling. My kids left with him. It seemed like I would never see them again. Then it became clear that the war in Vietnam was ending. My now ex-husband wrote me a poignant letter telling me he didn't think he would get out alive. I still cared about him and wondered what would happen to my kids as well.[2] I lost every single thing that truly mattered to me, including my self-respect.[3] Faced with the only acceptable option to relieve that agony I took up the practice of zazen. With the pain of these losses, every time I sat down on the cushion I burst into tears.

After I'd been struggling with doing zazen on my own for about a year and a half, in 1975 I was back in the United States for a couple months to do some work for one of my old clients. With nothing to do in the evening, I was in a bookstore. In those days there were maybe five books on Zen, and so, I picked up one of them and felt this sudden jiggle in my brain. I bought the book, went back to where I was staying, sat down, opened the book at random, and I happened to land on a page describing an incident that supposedly happened in Hakuin's life.

---

2   At the last minute, he was handed a ticket and he'd already sent my older son back to Turkey. My younger son at the time was staying with his grandmother and grandfather in North Carolina.

3   This type of life crisis is known as a "shamanic initiation" whose purpose appears to rip away the old to make room for the new, and that's exactly what it did.

Decades later when I was living in Japan and training at Sōgen-ji, I learned that the incident, while it was true, had not happened to Hakuin, but rather to his "grandfather" in his Zen lineage, Shidō Bunan. The story was of a middle-aged monk in Japan in an era before the Meiji Restoration changed the entire status of monks in that country. Prior to that time, monks were celibate and respected as people who had committed their life to spiritual practice. But in this seaside village, where this monk lived in his own tiny temple, a young, unmarried girl became pregnant. This was an extremely negative experience for the family and the village. The girl refused, at first, to name the father. Under pressure, she claimed it was the monk. Thus, when the baby was born, it was brought to the monk to raise since it was assumed to be his child. Though he knew it wasn't his child, he recognized that if the girl said he was the father, there could be no arguing with that. He received the infant and raised it for a year, at which point the mother confessed who the father really was.

What was amazing was that the monk's response to both the presentation of the baby and the return of the baby a year later was a simple, humble expression, impossible to translate accurately into English.[4] The flavor of it was a complete lack of ego investment and any desired results. His response came forth from a place of total freedom. It was a humble expression of profound acceptance. He felt no need to argue. He felt no anger at being wrongly accused. He was free to work clearly and effectively with the circumstances as they unfolded without any felt need to have it different. He expressed the same freedom from any felt need for anger or retribution. He was simply so incredibly free, that even though the year of raising the baby was quite difficult for him because the village scorned him and would not provide him with food, still he harbored no ill feelings.

As I read that, I plummeted into Shidō Bunan's mind state of profound liberation. I don't know how long I remained in that mind state, but when I came to, I had tears of joy streaming down my face. Although at the time I had no idea what had happened to me, I realized decades later that I had opened a window into true reality.

---

4   Literally, the Japanese phrase "so, ka" can be translated as "is that so?" But when Westerners say "is that so?" they don't normally say it with the same sense as it would have in Japanese; in the West, the expression is more often spoken from a place of defense, while in Japan it is an expression of profound acceptance.

Because the person in Turkey who had taught me zazen happened to be connected with the Rochester Zen Center, I called up to ask if I could talk to Roshi Kapleau about that mysterious experience. I was told that I would have to come to a workshop first, and then, afterwards, I would be able to speak with the roshi. I extended my stay in order to go to the upcoming workshop. Afterwards I was able to meet with Roshi Kapleau and describe what happened. Roshi questioned me with deep attention, paused, and responded, "That book is not a very good translation. If you want to read about Hakuin, read Yampolsky's *The Zen Master Hakuin*."[5]

I dutifully bought the book and found it incredibly boring. But the experience had hooked me and I continued my attempts to do zazen. At a certain point, I realized that to be able to do ongoing, regular Zen practice, I would have to go somewhere where I was forced to do it. I was able to move to Rochester and after a long wait was accepted to live at RZC, where I practiced under Roshi Kapleau for twenty intensive years until he retired. Two years later, after working with Bhodin Kjolhede Roshi, I met Harada Shōdō Roshi when he came to visit the Rochester Zen Center. Instantly a deep connection was felt. Coincidentally, someone gifted me a sesshin with Harada Roshi later that year when he came to the United States again. Not long afterwards I had the opportunity to go to Japan for three months. I spent the first two months at Sōgen-ji, two weeks in Kyoto sitting with Morinaga Soko Roshi, went to the Rohatsu sesshin at Bukkoku-ji under Harada Tangen Roshi, and came back to Kyoto briefly before returning to the United States filled with determination to train full time at Sōgen-ji. Counting a sesshin in Rochester, the sesshin with Harada Roshi in the United States, two osesshin and four kosesshin at Sōgen-ji, and the Rohatsu sesshin at Bukkoku-ji, it was an incredibly deep, concentrated, and valuable intensive training period. A few months later, I went to the next sesshin Harada Roshi led in the United States and continued on to Japan to take up full time residential training at Sōgen-ji.

I continued training with Harada Roshi up until the Covid pandemic struck; in other words, another twenty years of intensive

---

5   *The Zen Master Hakuin*, Philip Yampolsky, Columbia University Press, 1973.

spiritual deepening. Although, forty-some years before when I attempted to take up Zen training for the first time, zazen had been extremely difficult to do, by the time about four years had passed in residential training, it was no longer as difficult as I experienced greater and greater freedom as a result of the practice.

Although, in my case, practice was quite challenging when I began doing it, for many people who sit down for the first time to do zazen it's kind of a new and interesting adventure. Zen practice has an exciting hype in the West, or at least in America, and so it's kind of cool to be a Zen student. For some others of us, it's our only option as we're pushed against a wall in our life. For those of us in that latter category, it can be grueling, but since we have no other option, we take a deep breath and dive into the challenge. We learn how to sit in different meditation positions and go for it. As we begin to walk this Path, we are assigned a practice that has the potential to take us very deep. In Japanese it's called susok'kan; at Mountain Gate we translate it as extending the outbreath. It's a powerful grounding practice that can bring us eventually to an awakening. Once we have become sufficiently centered through the susok'kan, we have the option[6] to take up koan practice.[7]

After some time of working on the extended outbreath, we begin to realize the challenge that we have taken on. Zen practice begins to thin out the seemingly protective misperceptions we engage in as a result of an investment in a self-image, the product of conditioning. As this begins to happen, more clear awareness arises of our patterns of speech and behavior. We can mistakenly conclude that we're becoming worse people because of the practice. But, in reality, we're seeing more clearly how we behave. For Zen students willing to go forward into that, it offers the chance to investigate the origin of those patterns and work with that until those negative habits begin to dissolve and our behavior changes in positive ways.

One fellow Zen teacher I know calls the beginning of this phase, "the shit hitting the fan." Shunryu Suzuki Roshi, founder of San Francisco Zen Center, called it "mind weeds." He pointed out

---

6   With the approval of our teacher. In my experience, it is absolutely essential that we work with a genuine Rinzai teacher if we're going to be doing koan practice. Otherwise, we can seriously mislead ourselves.

7   See "koan" in the glossary.

that these mind weeds could be used to fertilize our practice. This is where the real practice begins. Zazen (Zen meditation) will uncover where we are caught and bring it to our own attention. As someone emerging from a sesshin at the Rochester Zen Center commented, "Zen is truly bodhisattvic. First it shows us where we're caught; and then it sets us free." When I say where we are caught, I mean where we have fixed ideas about ourselves resulting from our conditioning. If we've been traumatized, it can bring up flashbacks and intense memories, at which point it would be wise to seek the services of an experienced trauma therapist. Zen is very powerful medicine but, in those particular cases, it's important to get additional support from a trauma therapist. The two can go hand in hand beautifully and one can make much faster progress in both Zen practice and therapy if you're doing them at the same time regardless of whether you feel traumatized or not, as you've read in previous chapters. A number of therapists have confirmed that.

Experiences result in conditioning. If they've been negative experiences, we have usually drawn conclusions about ourselves that are not positive. But in order to give the appearance of being "normal" and "acceptable" we try to deny those self-appraisals and drive them out of our conscious mind. Nonetheless, they function in the background, influencing our behavior without our realizing it. We don't want to see it, we don't want to recognize it, because it's not comfortable and can even be painful and frightening. Human beings have a deep need to belong in the human family. In ancient times, if you weren't part of the clan, you'd likely not survive. Taking down a mastodon required a number of hunters working together to kill that huge animal. This is also why "shunning" is such a powerfully effective means of control. There's deep motivation for people to act in ways that will seem acceptable to whatever group they're in.[8] For that reason, it might be difficult for us to acknowledge that our behavior might be unacceptable and thus we hide it from ourselves.

This is normally a result of our conclusions about our personal worth and acceptability to the group we are born into. It's very

---

8 Of course, within many groups, there may still be people who "act out." This can be seen as the desperate need of a person who feels out of the group to gain attention in order to be accepted into the group, which is a strategy that often does not work.

telling that the Uvalde shooter, who came into a grade school and massacred students and teachers, had been bullied a great deal of his life and it sounds like he'd had a very unpleasant, non-supportive childhood as well from what little we can glean from the newspapers. Sadly, it's a combination of factors that lead a person to relieve their own suffering by causing intense suffering in others.

What causes the shit to hit the fan is our beginning to see clearly our misperceptions and the mind states that underlie those misperceptions. In practicing Zen, it's a gift when those mind weeds spring up and we choose to engage in the long maturation, which process will support the path to awakening. It's very uncomfortable and we begin to think what's really happening is that, rather than the Zen practice being supportive and bringing us to awakening, it's actually making us worse people. It's not true. It's only showing us more clearly how we behave. As you've read in previous chapters and in *Deepening Zen: The Long Maturation, Book One*, these self-misperceptions develop as a result of poor parenting or traumatic events unfollowed by compassionate support.

This is not something that needs to be judged, although we do judge it, because most of us have spent a good part of our life judging and being judged. At the very least we get grades in school. Sometimes in the interest of raising children who are "ideal" and reflect a parent's abilities, our parents, misguided, treat us in ways that no child should ever be treated. Through their own difficult situations, parents may not nurture children in ways that children need to be nurtured and supported. All of that can come up for us if we do serious zazen. Sadly, in response, some people, misunderstanding the process, choose to flee in search of alternative practices that can initially feel liberating. A small percentage of those people who do flee eventually come back to Zen practice five, ten, fifteen years later with renewed faith and commitment.

When I was head monitor,[9] there was a young man who came to sit his first sesshin, but the next morning he had vanished. The

---

9   The various Zen Buddhist groups in Asia and the West do not have identical terms for the leadership duties within the zendo. When Roshi Kapleau returned from Japan, he felt that Zen practice would never take off in the United States unless it was Westernized. So, he changed the vocabulary. The Rochester Zen Center's way of doing sesshin was to have two people called monitors in charge of the zendo, and one person in charge of the timing of periods of sitting zazen and kinhin.

rule at the Rochester Zen Center in those days was that if somebody leaves without permission in a sesshin then they are not allowed to come back to a sesshin ever again. Yet, I had a sense that this young man had a genuine vow for spiritual awakening. Four years later he applied for sesshin again. Because I had that faith in him, I did not remind the teacher that this young man had abandoned sesshin abruptly earlier. He was accepted to this sesshin.

The second evening of that sesshin, I found him in a crumpled heap outside the door to my room. In anguish he told me that he had done everything he could do to make it impossible for himself to leave this time. He had had his wife drive him; he left his wallet and keys at home; it was an era before cell phones so he had no way of calling anyone. I brought him in so we could talk and he decided to continue on despite the fear and anguish that had come up for him. Because he was willing to work with those feelings, he stayed through the entire sesshin, and at the end was ready to come to another.

There was another member of the Rochester Zen Center who had been to many sesshin but only to four days of any of those sesshin. When I asked him why he only went to four days of sesshin instead of all seven he said that it was on the fourth day that the terror came up. As we spoke, he decided to go to the upcoming sesshin for the full seven days. On the fourth day I could see him literally shaking on his cushion but he stuck it out and at the end of sesshin he was ecstatic.

There is anywhere between a bump and a mountain that can come up for us in practice. Often it will come up on the third or the fourth day of a sesshin. Generally, the first day is one of relative ease as we get our sea legs back and adjust to the sesshin schedule. During the second day we are pretty well adjusted to the physical challenge and now the mental and emotional challenges arise. By the end of the third day usually that roller coaster ride has begun to flatten out a bit and we're able to get to deeper work. It doesn't always happen that way. If what comes up is simply a tickle and not super compelling, it's best to ignore it rather than allow it to distract us from deepening the practice. But, if it's strong, by using the felt sense and choosing to go into the energy of it, even if it's a feeling of blankness we'll start to work through it to uncover what is deeper.

Metaphorically, through this process we are turning the fire-breathing dragons into little mice that scamper away. This allows us to begin to "unweave the tapestry" that caused us to be stuck in the first place. In this way we walk forward in deepening our practice. As we continue to progress, initially, sporadic moments of clarity and a feeling of spaciousness can come forth. And then can come the "ego backlash." It can surprise us when we've reached that increasing clarity that we could seem to go backwards. But it's pretty typical for a long time as the part of us that fears becoming truly free comes more to the fore and tries to stall the practice. Suddenly we can feel we've taken a huge step backwards but what's really happening is that the part of us that longs for liberation is temporarily being pushed back by the part of us that fears change. Prevail, and the highs and lows will diminish.

Because of all of this, it's useless to predict what's going to happen in a given sesshin or even within a sesshin at a given moment. It will karmically unfold as you gradually open towards that freedom.

流

Chapter Fourteen
A Sufi Teaching Story

Here's a teaching story from the Sufi tradition relevant to Zen practice. This is from *Tales of the Dervishes* by Idries Shah[1] and this particular one is called "The Tale of the Sands." These teaching stories are always metaphors. They're not specifically spelled out but they're used as ways to contemplate and ultimately reach a different place, a deeper place, of awareness and freedom.

> A stream, from its source in far-off mountains, passing through every kind and description of countryside, at last reached the sands of the desert. Just as it had crossed every other barrier, the stream tried to cross this one, but it found that as fast as it ran into the sand, its waters disappeared.
>
> It was convinced, however, that its destiny was to cross this desert, and yet there was no way. Now a hidden voice, coming from the desert itself, whispered: "The Wind crosses the desert, and so can the stream."
>
> The stream objected that it was dashing itself against the sand, and only getting absorbed; that the wind could fly, and this was why it could cross a desert.
>
> "By hurtling in your own accustomed way you cannot yet get across. You will either disappear or become a marsh. You must allow the wind to carry you over to your destination."
>
> But how could this happen? "By allowing yourself to be absorbed in the wind."

---

1 *Tales of the Dervishes*, Idries Shah, ISF Publishing, 2019, pg. 22-23.

This idea was not acceptable to the stream. After all, it had never been absorbed before. It did not want to lose its individuality. And, once having lost it, how was one to know that it could ever be regained?

"The wind," said the sand, "performs this function. It takes up water, carries it over the desert, and then lets it fall again. Falling as rain, the water again becomes a river."

"How can I know that this is true?"

"It is so, and if you do not believe it, you cannot become more than a quagmire, and even that could take many, many years; and it certainly is not the same as a stream."

"But can I not remain the same stream that I am today?"

"You cannot in either case remain so," the whisper said. "Your essential part is carried away and forms a stream again. You are called what you are even today because you do not know which part of you is the essential one."

When he heard this, certain echoes began to arise in the thoughts of the stream. Dimly, he remembered a state in which he—or some part of him, was it?—had been held in the arms of a wind. He also remembered—or did he?—that this was the real thing, not necessarily the obvious thing, to do.

And the stream raised his vapour into the welcoming arms of the wind, which gently and easily bore it upwards and along, letting it fall softly as soon as they reached the roof of a mountain, many, many miles away... He reflected, "Yes, now I have learned my true identity."[2]

---

2   There's a commentary attached to the story, "This beautiful story is current in verbal tradition in many languages, almost always circulating among dervishes and their pupils. It was used in Sir Fairfax Cartwright's *Mystic Rose from the Garden of the King*, published in Britain in 1899. The present version is from Awad Afifi the Tunisian, who died in 1870."

A Sufi Teaching Story

In this story, the stream goes through a series of events, fascinating experiences, and challenges throughout its life. This typical way of being, of thinking and experiencing, brings the stream to a certain point, but then it reaches an edge. There is more life, but it is a life that goes beyond what came before and that goes beyond who came before. The stream then must let go in order to leave that former life into a new, more expanded, experience of Being. As French author André Gide wrote, "One does not discover new lands without consenting to lose sight of the shore for a very long time." The stream must let go of its current identity as a stream in order to move on in its Life.

So, let's go through that again. Here is a stream living fully in the realm of form and identified with being a stream—tumbling over rocks, getting caught in log jams, and continuing on until it reaches the sands of the desert. Then, no matter how hard it tries, it cannot cross the desert, which seems like a shocking and abrupt end to being a stream. At the end of our life, if we have not come to understand the true nature of Life, we'll find ourselves in the same state of mind as the stream: fearful of the end of "my" existence.

The same thing can happen during our earlier years of Zen practice. We have a hard time trusting until through deepening practice we have enough insights into the freedom afforded by our zazen. Until that time we are likely to go back and forth between doubting and moving forward. An example of this doubt and distrust came in my early years of doing zazen when I actually thought—quite wrongly—that Roshi Kapleau didn't know at all what he was talking about. Well, it turned out he really did. And, once I could let go enough to believe in myself, I could believe in his teaching, and realize the gift of being able to train with such a genuine teacher.

Though we are not a stream, we are a stream of Life. We can do what the stream in this fable did. We reach a point where death is upon us and we can deny it; or, we can accept the process, letting go of our investment in a self-identity. If we choose not to go in that direction, rather than what the stream did, we will continue to fight the sand, kicking and screaming, as Dylan Thomas wrote, "Rage, rage against the dying of the light."[3] Instead, in choosing to let go of

---

3 "Do Not Go Gentle into That Good Night" by Dylan Thomas.

the form we identify with, we are able to peacefully move on as our karma unfolds to take a new form in a new life. Both dying to this physical life and coming to awakening (which means dying to who we think we are) demand surrender just as the stream had to let go.

Zen practice requires surrender. The more we allow ourselves to let go through zazen, the more free we become. Thus, the more able we are to meet whatever adversity or pleasant experience comes forth to us, and not be attached to results, and not be dismayed, or upset, or horrified, or happy about results because we are unattached to how we think we need to be. This is not to say that you don't feel. It's not as if you've had a lobotomy. The narrowness of our life concerns and attachments, which is always limited by the self-image, drops. What has disappeared in those experiences is the narrowness of our fixations[4] on a personal view. Those fixations create a filter through which we see and experience. One way of viewing this is instead of trying to drink the ocean through a straw, suddenly you open to the extraordinary experience of the entire ocean unfiltered.

Through the process of the self-image putting down roots in our psyche, we lose track of our authenticity, and therefore the self-image begins to drive our behavior. Yet, at the end of our life, we will have no choice but to once again abandon the persona and dissolve into the Beingness of Life. If we have been able to let go sufficiently before that point, we will simply allow the wind to carry us into the next life. We won't try to hang on, forcing ourselves to remain a stream attempting to cross the sand. If we allow ourselves to relinquish that self-established identity, the challenging emotions that may come up for us will simply evaporate. This is accomplished by tuning in to the different energies in our body, the different sensations that come up when we feel upset, happy, concerned, traumatized, or whatever else.

It's a long process, but it's a very effective, positive process for becoming fully alive. As Flora Courtois saw in one of her visions: she was manipulating colored blocks in a gray, nondescript office. She suddenly turned around and saw through the window behind her an exuberant, colorful expression of Life. There was a small river

---

4 "Am I good enough?" "Do I have enough money?" "Do those people not like me?" "I can't do it." "Oh no, did I say the wrong thing?"

meandering through a meadow, butterflies flitting around the flowers, mountains and forests in the distance—all so exciting, so different from the gray environment she was used to being in! Excited, she opened the window and climbed out, immersing herself in that Reality. This is the difference between fully, freely experiencing life without the self-imposed blinders and remaining caught in a narrow, limited life.

In another metaphor, Indian Jesuit priest and psychotherapist Anthony De Mello (1931–1987) wrote there's a busload of people journeying through fascinating landscapes, forests, over hills, on a very long journey. They're chatting among themselves and they get to the end of the journey and it turns out the blinds have been down all the time they were traveling through those magnificent landscapes. They missed it all. As in Flora Courtois' vision of manipulating little blocks in a gray office, most people tend to go through life as William Blake so cogently wrote in his poem "London" with "mind-forg'd manacles," which is to say a self-imposed enslavement that begets blindness to the richness of life.[5]

The process of letting go and tuning into Reality, described in this chapter, is a profoundly effective way of becoming fully alive.

---

5   "In every cry of every Man, / In every Infants cry of fear, / In every voice: in every ban, / The mind-forg'd manacles I hear." "London" by William Blake.

Chapter Fifteen
Fruits of Advanced Zen Practice

To be able to encounter the Dharma, feel a connection, and draw towards it is an immense and rare gift. To have the karmic connection with a teacher and carve out time to enable that connection to flourish and start practicing is even more rare. There's a metaphor in Buddhism that discovering an affinity with Buddhist practice is like a sea turtle rising to the surface of the ocean only once every 500 years and, as it comes to the surface, its head happens to go through the knot-hole of a random piece of wood floating on the water. The coincidence of those two events happening at the same time—the surfacing of the sea turtle and its proximity to that one piece of wood floating on the vast ocean—expresses that rarity. So, we shouldn't discount our connection with practice, as challenging as it can be sometimes. It's profoundly valuable, filled with the potential to free us in immeasurable ways.

However, some people attracted to Zen have this idea that when we have practiced long and sufficiently enough to have a kensho[1] that our life will be all roses, no thorns. The assumption is that we won't have any problems after that, that we'll just sail smoothly along. On the contrary, challenges will continue to arise in our lives in accordance with our karma, but we have the option to be free of attachment to results, and thus move through those challenges with ease, clarity, and innate wisdom rather than worry and anxiety. But it takes time. You don't just sit on the cushion once, lightning strikes, and you're home free. It's imperative to work on the long maturation throughout our Zen practice in order to develop the basis to support those insights and awakening experiences throughout day-to-day

---

[1] "Kensho" literally means "seeing into" the true nature of reality. While significant, it tends to be relatively superficial. "Satori" is considered a deeper level. But it is the deepest level of Awakening that will make us considerably more free.

life. Unless this ongoing work is undertaken, a kensho will become nothing more than a nice memory.

An experience of kensho comes with an expansive sense of freedom, but unless the work of the long maturation is ongoing that sense of freedom will fade. As we continue practicing, awareness of our habit patterns will arise over time as we gain insight into where we are caught. In response to that, if we don't engage in the vital process of the long maturation, those habit patterns, although somewhat weakened, will remain lodged in our psyche. Following an insight, after a time, which will be longer or shorter depending on how deep that insight was, the old habit patterns will come rolling back in and we will not be free of them despite what it had felt like. We'll go on behaving in the same old pain-producing ways. I have known people who, after a kensho, have even been able to pass subsequent koans, yet whatever dysfunctional behavior was there before had not changed. They had not recognized the importance of working to dislodge those negative patterns.

As an example, in the 1960s, a man came to visit Roshi Kapleau. This man had been a soldier in the invasion of Normandy in the second World War. In a pivotal moment in 1944, as thousands of Allied soldiers—mainly American, Canadian, and British troops—jumped out of their landing craft at the Normandy beaches, they were met with a barrage of enemy fire. Although the Allies' attack was ultimately successful the losses were heavy. At the end of the war, this veteran returned to the United States in a deep state of anguish. All he could do was wander the streets of New York City, bumping into people, light poles, and trash cans, completely absorbed in questioning: how could such suffering exist, how could people be so brutal? That focused search resulted in a kensho.[2] But, having no way to deepen it and have that understanding inform his behavior from then on through the ongoing process of the long maturation,

---

2   To be clear, that kensho could not have come from intellectual questioning. The existential quest often begins with an intellectual question, which then has to be moved beyond if the search is to bear fruit. Instead, to reach kensho, satori, or even deeper awakening requires a profound, nameless search. It is crucial that one's self-created identity disappears as the importance of the nameless search itself becomes greater than the maintenance of a personal self-image. One has to completely forget oneself. This is why when we get close to this point in our practice fear can come up: a fear that we will lose control, a fear that we will disappear, a fear that we will die. In reality it is only the skewed self-image that will disappear, at least temporarily.

by the time this man went to see Roshi Kapleau that insight and its accompanying joy was only a dim memory. Had he had access to guidance to do that work at the time, that insight could have deepened infinitely and truly transformed his life.

So, what does the long maturation look like for a Zen student? I was already a senior student working my way through the koan curriculum and serving as Head of Zendo—the position just below the teacher—at the Rochester Zen Center, when I began to realize for the first time that my communication with others had often been expressed in a demeaning and confrontational tone. Part of the duties as Head of Zendo, especially during a sesshin, was to encourage but also to correct sangha members. Sesshin at Rochester is carried on in absolute silence. Communication is minimal and accomplished by writing a note. If the need for communication came up, I would first consider whether a note was necessary, whether it was helpful, and how to write it in a supportive tone. Then I would write the note, pass it to the second monitor, ask that person to read it and give me feedback on it, and taking that feedback to heart, would usually rewrite the note before I gave it to the person it was meant for. Although at that time I had never heard the term "the long maturation," I much later realized that's what I had been doing.

If we don't do that work, we will unwittingly continue to create suffering for ourselves and others. In actuality, depending on our karma, difficulties and challenges may still arise. Nonetheless, if we have seen deeply enough, we will be far less caught by those seemingly negative experiences. If we go deeper yet, into what can really be considered a profound Awakening and all along work on the long maturation, then there will be no friction in our encounters with difficult circumstances.

As Harada Roshi described it when he experienced that level of awakening, "I realized all I have to do is simply to receive whatever comes to me." By that he meant that the expansive clarity and liberation that he opened to had resulted in the ongoing ability to not get caught by anything but from within that clarity to respond in exactly the right way. That level of lack of attachment translates to what is expressed in Case 6 in the *Hekiganroku*, also known as the *Blue Cliff Record*:

Ummon addressed the assembly and said, "I am not asking you about the days before the fifteenth of the month.[3] But what about after the fifteenth? Come and give me a word about those days." And he himself gave the answer for them: "Every day is a good day."[4]

When we step out of our own way, when we drop those "mind-forg'd manacles,"[5] whatever happens it doesn't cause us fear, trepidation, anguish, upset, or, in a word, suffering. Like Ummon comments, every day is a good day regardless of what challenges arise. And this is not Pollyanna speaking. Suffering is caused by an attachment to a persona and an attachment to a result. If neither of those attachments exists there's nothing to trigger suffering. A committed Zen practice, continued for however long it takes, will bring us to that point in our life.[6]

Here's a personal story to illustrate what years of intensive Zen training can do for us. I'd been living and training at the Rochester Zen Center full time for about two years when I was driving in our brand-new Volkswagen Rabbit and turned left at a green light with nothing in view coming from the opposite direction. Suddenly a large car sped down the hill, did not attempt to slow down, and struck the Volkswagen. The force of the blow to the rear tire caused the car to spin around and slam backwards into another car. As a relatively new Zen student I felt I should be calm, cool, and collected in the face of that crash. But, instead, I sat there shaking uncontrollably. Full of shame and self-condemnation, I wondered, "How could I have done such a thing?!" Even though it was the other driver's fault (it was only February but he had already had three accidents that year!), the self-condemnation was a deeply ingrained assumption as a result of my childhood experiences that I was always the guilty one. Eventually, I was able to make my way back home in the crippled car. For the next two days I remained quite shaken and in shock.

---

3   Ummon is using "the fifteenth of the month" as a metaphor for Awakening.
4   *Two Zen Classics: Mumonkan & Hekiganroku*, translated with commentaries by Katsuki Sekida, pg. 161.
5   See "William Blake" in Chapter 14.
6   This includes the work of the long maturation.

Fast forward fifty years later, having done intensive training most of the intervening years. I was driving home in our twenty-year-old truck when, coming over a rise, the New Mexico afternoon sun completely blinded me. I realized that I had driven off the road onto the edge of a ravine where at least one driver had previously gone over and died. I was fully aware but I felt no fear. Whatever would be would be. There was no anxiety, nor was I dissociating. I remained fully present throughout the experience. I gently turned the steering wheel, avoiding the ravine, but effectively rolled the truck. As the truck rolled over, I was so one with it that it was simply a fascinating experience. Again, there was no fear. Because of the pressure of my weight hanging against the seat belt I was unable to release it and hung there waiting for somebody to notice the accident. Two men from a neighboring village happened to come by. They were able to cut the seatbelt and I crawled out the busted back window. The head of our volunteer fire department, a friend and neighbor, arrived moments later. He examined me and confirmed that I was neither injured nor in shock. As cell phone service is often spotty in that part of New Mexico, he quickly brought back the command car from the nearby station a few hundred yards away in order to call off the ambulance via a radio call.

The two bales of hay I had bought tumbled out of the truck with the accident. I sat on one as our emergency volunteers began to arrive. One of them brought his truck and was able to drive the hay bales the mile and a half to Mountain Gate. Two young policemen arrived to take a report. They recognized that I had not been speeding and didn't charge me with any traffic infractions. When I returned to Mountain Gate, our sesshin continued.

Whereas in the earlier accident, the Volkswagen was repairable, in this case the truck was a total loss leaving us with no vehicle at all for months. But we adjusted until we would be able to purchase a replacement vehicle. I would deal with that with no problem. The contrast between my reaction to the two accidents, in neither of which I nor anyone else was injured, was, I am sure, due to all the intervening years of intensive Zen practice.

My story of the freeing benefits of Zen practice is certainly not unique to me. Roshi Philip Kapleau intuitively understood the need for deepening a realization and bringing it to life in his own behavior. He worked relentlessly on this into his peaceful dying just three months before his 92nd birthday. The entire time I trained with Roshi Kapleau, which was more than twenty years, I witnessed again and again his commitment to the work of the long maturation.

The second year I was attending him in Mexico as he was writing his book *The Zen of Living and Dying: A Practical and Spiritual Guide*,[7] we had rented a two-storey house in a small town called Tepoztlan on the other side of the mountains from Mexico City. The second storey of the house was accessed only by a long, outdoor, rough, brick stairway. Roshi lived on the second floor. His attendants, a Mexican sangha member and I, lived on the first floor. It was a Sunday evening and the Mexican attendant was visiting with her family while I was attending the roshi who had done a renewal of marriage vows for two Mexican sangha couples in Mexico City. It was early April and the couples had given him a plate of the first of the highly prized Manila mangos of the year. When we got back to Tepoztlan, he headed upstairs with his plate of mangoes, then having second thoughts decided to share them. He started back down the long, brick stairway.

We hadn't realized it yet, but Roshi was in the early stages of Parkinson's Disease and tended to imperceptibly drag one of his feet. His foot caught on the brick stairway and he tumbled all the way down to the landing. When I heard the crash of the plate shattering, I ran out and found him in shock lying on the landing surrounded by the scattered mangos. The roshi was small and thin and quite light of weight, so I was able to get him to the car where he lay down in the back seat, silent. I drove him to the local medical clinic. However, the young intern who was there had no x-ray or other equipment that could diagnose broken bones. He could only offer a pain killer. He took us to a local doctor who was able to hook Roshi up to an IV and determine that he had broken his wrist, and said now we needed to take him to the Red Cross hospital in Cuernavaca.

I drove the fourteen slow miles to Cuernavaca with Roshi lying in the backseat, his head in the doctor's lap as the doctor held up

---

7   *The Zen of Living and Dying: A Practical and Spiritual Guide*, Philip Kapleau, Shambhala, 1998.

the IV bottle. We stopped on the way at the home of Gerardo Gally, then the head of Casa Zen, the Mexican sangha. The stop was necessary because Gerardo did not have a telephone so stopping by was the only way I could alert him to what happened.

By the time we reached the hospital it was midnight on Sunday evening and the small staff on duty immediately took Roshi into the x-ray room. They wouldn't allow me into the room, but seconds later they rushed out and announced they would not do anything further until the morning when the full staff was there. Roshi had had some form of life-threatening arrest. Two years earlier, he had just gone through a surgery in Santa Fe, New Mexico and given a standard painkiller for that type of surgery. The painkiller had caused him to suddenly stop breathing, commonly known as a pulmonary arrest, and so, I was aware of his sensitivity to pain medication. At the local clinic in Tepoztlan, we had examined the list of contents in the painkiller being offered to Roshi and found nothing of the same ingredients that had caused him to stop breathing in Santa Fe. So, Roshi had decided to take that painkiller, which may have been what had triggered the arrest at the Red Cross hospital.

Roshi spent the night in a bed in a regular hospital room. I spent the night in a chair in his room and one of his local sangha members slept on the floor outside the room so that we could stop anybody from giving him unknown medication. In the morning, Gerardo arrived with one of the Casa Zen sangha members, a doctor named Amelia Amaro, who had arranged for him to be treated at the Humana Hospital in Mexico City. We caravaned over the mountain to the hospital where, because of his history with reactions to medications, Roshi was interviewed by the anaesthesiologist extensively and in English before they took him in for more tests and subsequent surgeries. It turned out he had more broken bones. We spent several nights in that hospital before returning to Tepoztlan and then it was time for him to go back to the United States to where he was living in Santa Fe.

What was Roshi Kapleau's reaction to that whole extended experience? Although he was in significant pain for quite a long time, he received it with silent, absolute presence, and not a word of complaint. The extremity and pain that he'd gone through had simply not been a problem for him.

In another instance, years earlier, I was his attendant at a sesshin in New Mexico. The Rochester Zen Center at the time was following the classic Japanese training schedule where the year is separated into three-month quarters and the teacher is actively teaching for every other quarter. During those inactive periods Roshi would head for warmer climates in Costa Rica or Mexico. He had returned from those trips having ingested two separate strains of amoebas, which over time had caused him increasing intestinal discomfort. In addition, he was lactose intolerant and loved ice cream, which didn't help. One day in sesshin, I went in to meet him in his quarters and found him doubled over in silent agony. As if that weren't enough, it was the rainy season in New Mexico and the roof leaked into his room. Although we constantly moved his bed in an effort for him to escape the leaks, still, he woke up each night with water dripping on him. Again, no complaint. He was just totally at one with these circumstances.

A further example occurred in a sesshin in Mexico. We had rented out a four-hundred-year-old stone monastery/orphanage that had been turned into a sports club. Roshi was housed in what had become the dance studio. Again, he was subject to yet another leaky roof. It was February and there were very few electrical outlets in that centuries old building and so multiple extension cords had to be plugged together to reach 60 feet to his bed for his electric blanket. Mid sesshin, in the middle of the night, someone heading to the bathroom had tripped over the cord and unwittingly unplugged the electric blanket, leaving him to sleep the rest of the night in the wintry cold. During these multiple experiences, Roshi expressed no complaints. He simply received. Simply receiving, we are not caught in any ideas of personal comfort or other attachments. We are free to accommodate and adjust without any friction. He had let go enough in all his years of zazen that his "mind forg'd manacles" had essentially dropped away.

Years after that, Roshi Kapleau was formally diagnosed with Parkinson's Disease. The dying off of brain cells that produce dopamine, which is essential for movement, causes the increasing debilitation characteristic of Parkinson's. It was later discovered that long term use of the new medication he was given had a permanent side effect known as tardive dyskinesia. The result for Roshi was major uncontrollable movements, including spontaneously sticking out his tongue and, as it got worse, wildly waving his arms all the time, occasionally knocking off his glasses. As well, his voice became very, very soft and it was difficult to hear him speak. This went on for years. At one point, when I was visiting him near the end of his life, we simply sat in silent communion. We were in harmony and the energy between us was that of unconditional compassion and peace. With his arms still violently waving around and his tongue periodically sticking out, I said to him, "Roshi, this Parkinson's sure is a good teacher, isn't it?" He responded with a quiet and soft, "It sure is."

How many of us without that level of letting go could respond as Roshi did, just receiving?

One of the major benefits of advanced Zen practice—so long as we're committed to the long maturation—is that we are offered the chances to free ourselves from being caught in fear. Growing up, I had often awakened in terror from a nightmare in which I was suddenly falling. I would jerk myself awake each of those times. When I got to the Rochester Zen Center and was training there for a while, the nightmares returned. It was annoying because the schedule at the Center was such that one didn't get a lot of sleep, and to have that sleep interrupted by this recurrent nightmare was definitely unwanted. I thought to myself, "this is only a dream, let's see what happens if I let the dream continue." So, the next time the dream came, I let it continue. As I started to fall, however, I fainted, effectively stopping the nightmare. The next time I had the nightmare, I felt myself falling off a high cliff next to the ocean. I could clearly see the large, black boulders down below. Allowing myself to fall, I suddenly realized mid-fall that whether I died, dashed against the boulders at the bottom, or survived, there would be absolutely no difference, that Life would not stop. It would flow on unhindered. That realization was indescribably liberating. My view of Life and the meaning of death radically changed. I never had the dream again.

When I was in Japan in training at Sōgen-ji, the Kobe earthquake, one of the most violent earthquakes at near a ten in the

Richter scale, took place. Sōgen-ji was located only 90 miles from the epicenter, so a great deal of the intensity of that earthquake was transmitted through the ground beneath Sōgen-ji. Although it was not my first earthquake it was the most intense one I'd experienced. It felt like the temple was sitting on top of a giant jackhammer, jumping violently up and down. We discovered later that the large columns, originally centered on their stone foundations to hold up the structure of the hondo—the huge building where ceremonies traditionally took place and where we did the morning chanting—were jolted to the point where they were overhanging a couple inches off the edge of those foundations. In the bell tower, the huge, heavy bell had swung so wildly around that the columns supporting it had split, requiring them later to be fitted with iron straps.

I was jisharyo at the time and in those days it was the jisharyo's duty to end morning sanzen before breakfast. So, I had returned to the student waiting area after my own sanzen until the proper time to announce "sanzen is over," at which point everyone would return to the zendo to await the breakfast bell. It was also my duty to take care of people who had become ill or otherwise needed help. As the violent earthquake began with a subtle rattling of the glass panes of the shoji panels that formed the exterior walls of the building and continued to increase in intensity, I was not yet sure whether to get everyone out of the building or not.[8] This earthquake was increasing in force longer than other earthquakes I had experienced. Coincidentally, years earlier, I had worked at the Earthquake Institute in Turkey and was well versed in the behavior of earthquakes.[9] The roshi rang his handbell indicating that sanzen was continuing regardless of the violent quaking. There was my answer. We would all stay and go to sanzen. The temple did not collapse, but all the contents of the cupboards in the kitchen fell out. When I returned to the zendo it was to a surreal scene: everyone sitting silently absorbed in their

---

[8] I was not yet sure because, in my experience, when the time is right to do something, I feel a wordless sense indicating a direction and an action that, although not necessarily logical, has always been the right thing to do. No doubt this sense is a result of long years of Zen practice. Zen meditation in general winnows out the "mind weeds" to allow clearer perception. Even if that sense has not yet arrived, it's only because it's not yet time to take action.

[9] Turkey, like Japan, sits on a belt of seismic activity.

practice, surrounded by all the things that had toppled out of the cupboards above the tans.

People reading this chapter may wonder, wasn't it reckless and dangerous to continue sanzen as the building was shaking and potentially collapsing? Wouldn't it have been safer to get people out of and away from the building? Unknown to most people reading this book, because Japan has functioned through centuries of earthquakes, Japanese architects and carpenters have long developed effective building techniques such that the buildings would survive these multiple earthquakes. For example, traditional temples and traditional houses are built with what is known as post-and-beam construction. To connect those posts and beams, Japanese carpenters had created many intricate joint patterns, thus building flexibility into the structure, making it much less liable to fall down in an earthquake. The buildings at Sōgen-ji, many of which date back to the fifteenth century, had been constructed with this technique. Certainly Roshi knew this and, having been born and raised in Japan, had experienced many earthquakes in his life. He understood that the danger was considerably less than people unfamiliar with earthquakes would have thought. This is to say that Roshi had a deep innate wisdom and clarity as well as a practical understanding of the situation with which to make an informed decision.

Like the falling nightmare I had that finally brought about a realization that what we call death is not the dreaded end of Life, as it's so typically assumed it is, certainly the roshi understood that as well. Of course, we experience grief at the loss of loved ones who die and this is normal. But Harada Roshi, in his wisdom, was offering his students an opportunity to confront a fear of death and, through confronting it, to awaken to the true nature of reality, which he himself had experienced long before. As I had recognized in that dream of falling off the cliff, there is no difference between Life and death. Life will forever go on. But human beings are so fearful that our seemingly protective self-image, which we mistakenly think of as our true self will disappear, that we tend to fear death. In reality, of course as its karma dissolves, this body will die, and with it the fake self. But the Beingness that we are can never die. Although this may seem difficult to understand, it is the deepest Truth.

My brother Bill had given hints for some years toward the end of his life that he was curious about what happens after death. As a medical doctor, seeing people die, whether they were his patients or not, seems to have led him into a deep, quiet exploration of what it means. When he was about 70 years old, he was diagnosed with bladder cancer. He was not a smoker and he was in excellent health so the prognosis was excellent. Because he was in such good health, he was given a double dose of chemotherapy prior to a ten-and-a-half-hour surgery that was supposed to take care of the problem. Six weeks after the fourth post-surgery dose of chemo he was dead. We had not realized how aggressive that cancer was.

I was on my way to Denver when I got a call from one of my sisters saying that Bill had told his wife it was time to let his sisters know he had very little time left. Shocked, I pulled over to the side of the road and called him. He said, "I've had a good life. I have no regrets." I was two years older than him and growing up together we were very close, but I was also envious of him. I said to him over the phone, "I'm sorry for all the grief I gave you when we were growing up." He laughed. I told him I wouldn't be able to come to see him until Monday. It was Friday that day and he lived in Virginia. He said, "I won't be here then." And indeed, the morning after I returned from Denver, I received a call from one of my sisters telling me he had just passed. It was Monday morning.

What I experienced then was about four hours of a mild form of grief and puzzlement. I realized I had tuned into my brother's mind state. That was followed by about eighteen hours of a mind state that is impossible to be described in words. The closest I can get to describing it is "luminous transparency." There was an enormous sense of liberation. After about eighteen more hours, it gradually faded and I knew he had moved on. I had no doubt that my brother had experienced a profound awakening due to his willingness to walk into his own experience of dying without any preconceived ideas about it.

We don't have to wait for the approach of our own death to have that same level of realization. As my brother did, we can walk with openness and utter presence into whatever comes up for us as we dare to peer over and leap off the edge of that cliff. This has the potential to give us the same depth of freedom and subsequent transformation of our life[10] as we sit on our cushion in the zendo.

---

10 Assuming we continue with the long maturation.

Chapter Sixteen
Post Sesshin Advice

Today is the seventh and final day of this sesshin, but hopefully it is only the jumping off place for everyone's practice to deepen further. Ultimately, if we do that work of deepening, we will become more and more at ease in our lives, fractured relationships will begin to smooth out, and the general friction felt in life will begin to fall away. Of course in the earlier years we are so accustomed to judging that we'll misjudge the results of our zazen out of a host of misperceptions. At the end of our early sesshins we may emerge with a sense of failure, especially if we had assumed we'd experience kensho. Initially, sesshin can feel to most people like a project that will make them special and unique, that they'll come out with a sense of accomplishment, sporting a halo and yet another boy scout badge. However, Zen practice is about removing the need for halos and badges. The process of sesshin, which is to say of fully engaged zazen, will begin to bring into clearer focus what our customary business typically obscures, namely a belief that we're not good enough, that we're not lovable, that we're not worthy. And so at the end of sesshin your mind may be filled with the anguish of those false beliefs. But with each succeeding sesshin, beliefs will be revealed as what they really are—false views and patterns shaped by childhood conditioning and the pressures of society's narrow views and expectations.

In my first several years of frequent sesshin at the Rochester Zen Center, when the other sesshin participants headed out into the zendo foyer after the ending ceremony, I would slink down the back stairway, metaphorically crawl through the basement, and come up, avoiding the happy crowd, head through the Link Building over to the reception area and pull out an application for the next sesshin. As I filled in the application, I'd think to myself, "Are you nuts?! You want to go through that again?!" Luckily, I had realized some time earlier that for me there was no alternative. Not to punish myself again and again, but to enter the pain with the clear understanding that it was the only way to become liberated from it. If I remember right, that whole second full year of sesshin after sesshin at RZC, I had cried my way through each entire seven-day event filled with self-pity and deep loneliness—in a word, anguish.

After that year I no longer needed to do that. It seemed my practice had been deepening regardless of what it felt like. And this is important. Persistence is vital, regardless of whether you feel like you're progressing or not. I was encouraged when Roshi Kapleau, during a teisho, shared a letter he'd asked one of his students to write describing a kensho they had had in a previous sesshin. This anonymous woman wrote, "When I entered the zendo at the beginning of that sesshin, I had to virtually nail myself to the mat. The last thing I wanted to do was walk into that sesshin. It was a struggle to stay there. But, in the end, I realized that this practice is truly bodhisattvic—*first it shows you where you're caught* and then it sets you free." Hearing that account while still in the stage of being shown where I was caught, I clung to that woman's story as a ray of hope and encouragement.

But zazen was still challenging until just a few years later when I was passed on my breakthrough koan. Things changed radically at that point, not because I had been passed on my koan, but because I had become free enough and clear enough to be able to answer the koan. Subsequent koans refined and clarified my mind with the result that sesshins were no longer filled with despair. I became so much more at ease as the constraints of my misperceptions fell away.

Not everyone comes out of sesshin depressed, but enough of us do that it's important to mention this. Lacking the faith that they truly can become liberated, sadly some people stop practice altogether. The pain that we come to zazen to get rid of will surface during zazen, which can be daunting and disappointing, but in reality, it offers us the distinct opportunity to work through our attachment to it, pulling it out by the roots. I want to emphasize that it is an attachment as many of us find comfort in our identity as one who suffers. If you do a cost-benefit analysis of this self-image of pain, you may well discover why it is so comforting to hold onto it and what that tenacity has cost you. Discovering that can be very helpful in working to dissolve the source of that attachment. Perseverance is key.

With concentrated zazen through seven days, we become more focused and more clear and more aware. We can have a taste of what American Transcendentalist author Ralph Waldo Emerson describes when he writes, "even in the mud and scum of things, something always, always sings." In other words, we experience more of the actual richness of color, sound, and sensation, than when our mind is full of the distractions of daily life. After sesshin, as we re-enter society, this unaccustomed richness can seem overwhelming. However, if we have grounded ourselves in that rich experience—and this is a result of more advanced practice—it can be as Emerson said. As we move more deeply into our practice, we may experience sporadic moments in which we can hear the song in the midst of what would ordinarily be perceived as disgusting.

And it's possible to go even further into this openness, which Alice Walker seems to describe in her novel, *The Color Purple*:

> Here's the thing, say Shug. The thing I believe. God is inside you and inside everybody else. You come into the world with God. But only them that search for it inside find it. And sometimes it just manifest itself even if you not looking, or don't know what you looking for. Trouble do it for most folks, I think. Sorrow, Lord. Feeling like shit.
> It? I ast.
> Yeah, It. God ain't a he or a she, but a It.
> But what do it look like? I ast.
> Don't look like nothing, she say. It ain't a picture show. It ain't something you can look at apart from anything else, including yourself. I believe God is everything, say Shug. Everything that is or ever was or ever will be. And when you can feel that, and be happy to feel that, you've found it.
>
> Shug a beautiful something, let me tell you. She frown a little, look out cross the yard, lean back in her chair, look like a big rose.

> She say, My first step from the old white man was trees. Then air. Then birds. Then other people. But one day when I was sitting quiet and feeling like a motherless child, which I was, it come to me: that feeling of being part of everything, not separate at all. I knew that if I cut a tree, my arm would bleed. And I laughed and I cried and I run all around the house. I knew just what it was.[1]

As you can see by the writings, accounts, and stories quoted throughout this book, enlightenment is not unique to Buddhism. It is not special. Everyone has the potential to open to this True reality and its inherent freedom. The uniqueness of Rinzai Zen Buddhist practice is that it provides the tools to access this potential and turn it into reality.

However, it's possible to dip our toe in during sesshin then, after, go back to live our lives as usual. In that case the benefits gained during sesshin will fade. But just recognizing that doesn't always make it easy to continue to deepen beyond sesshin in our daily life. As an example, the first sesshin I ever went to was a four-day sesshin. I had commuted to Rochester from out of the country with a simple goal: to survive the schedule. I did indeed survive the schedule and though the four days were quite challenging, the morning after the sesshin ended, when it's typical for people to sit in the zendo informally however long or short they want to, without realizing it I sat for two hours fully absorbed and without moving. But returning to where I was living at the time, I found that I could not bear to even cross the threshold into the room where my mat and cushion were. This continued for three weeks before I was finally able to force myself down on the cushion again. It's why I decided to move to Rochester to live at the Center, because then I would have to sit every day or I couldn't live there. I'm sharing this only to give you an idea that the early years of practice are difficult and it's not so easy to follow up on sesshin with continued sitting. Of course now, decades later, whether in sesshin or not, there's no difference in the level of my

---

[1] *The Color Purple*, Alice Walker, Penguin Books, 1987.

willingness to sit. I did persist and I'm so grateful that I did. My life is very different now, so much more free, so much more peaceful, so much happier.

That said, it helps a lot to be part of a sangha, our spiritual family, and enjoy the mutual support therein. Our society is so caught in power, a me-first perspective, and a narrow set of rules and regulations defining human worth, whereas being with our sangha family can provide an environment that does not equate self-worth with power, financial success, or whether or not you have more status and possessions than your neighbor.

So, after sesshin what can help maintain and enhance the work accomplished during that sesshin? It's important to note that the efforts in concentration and focus we develop during those seven days results in something termed *joriki*, which is the special concentration of energy that comes from that focused practice. At the end of sesshin, if we're not careful, we'll allow it to rapidly drain away through a lot of centrifugal activity. It can make us feel like superman able to "leap tall buildings in a single bound," but if we don't reign this energy in, about two days after sesshin ends we'll find ourselves sinking into malaise, lethargy, melancholy, or even depression. We can avoid that by taking the following steps for the next several weeks after sesshin.

1. Engage in physical activity. If you're a runner, go for a long run. Go to the gym and lift weights. Take a good hike in the forest. Or, as I did when I realized its benefit, get down on your hands and knees and scrub the floor for however long it takes to scrub the entire floor.
2. Get extra zazen.
3. Avoid high energy social situations for the next couple of weeks.
4. Get extra sleep. Most likely during sesshin you'll have built up a sleep debt. Doing that heavy exercise soon after sesshin will help you be able to sleep. For all of my early sesshin, I would lie awake so full of energy I was unable to go to

sleep yet desperately needed to sleep. It wasn't until that Sunday afternoon when I spent three hours scrubbing the floor that I recognized the immense benefit of physical activity post-sesshin.
5. Keep practicing. It is ongoing practice that will bring more lasting results.

Finally, as Khenchen Konchog Gyaltshen Rinpoche tells us in *Complete Guide to the Buddhist Path*,[2] "Unbroken practice is like a watchful guard. It is simply unscattered and is free from acceptance or rejection. There is no duality of things to be abandoned and their antidotes. This is my heart advice." Unbroken practice does not necessarily mean not to have experiences like the one I did where I couldn't face the cushion for three weeks. Unbroken practice is to persist regardless of these challenges and impediments. In other words, in our early years of practice, because of the load of conditioning we need to work through, there will be times when it is difficult to plop down on that cushion. There will be times when it can feel like we have to nail ourselves to the mat in a sesshin, but as we persist the practice will naturally deepen and become as Rinpoche said, "simply unscattered and...free from acceptance or rejection." Ultimately, there is no duality or separation between practice and regular life. Sesshin does not end and neither does your day-to-day life.

It is as written in the *Gospel of Thomas*, "Split a piece of wood; I am there. Lift up the stone, and you will find me there." Or, as Layman P'ang wrote, "My daily activities are not usual, I'm just naturally in harmony with them. Grasping nothing, discarding nothing, in every place there's no hindrance, no conflict. Who assigns the ranks of vermilion and purple? The hills' and mountains' last speck of dust is extinguished. My supernatural power and marvelous activity—drawing water and carrying firewood." As these quotes express, the simple activities of daily living, with ongoing deep zazen and the work of the long maturation, are experienced as they truly are, miraculous and extraordinary. This occurs as our self-image, that monkey on our back chattering in our ear, dissolves through long practice.

---

2 *Complete Guide to the Buddhist Path*, Kenchen Konchog Gyaltshen, Snow Lion, 2010.

Post Sesshin Advice

If you've ever seen a lotus blossom, and I don't mean a water lily, I mean an actual lotus blossom, which is large as a dinner plate and exquisite in its translucent quality and famous for its beauty, you'll understand why it's revered. This beautiful flower grows out of the mud. The flower's perfection and wholeness were always nascent in the roots nourished by the mud, just as we entering spiritual practice grow from the mud of our conditioned self-image. Through that practice, the purity and wholeness of who we always have been are revealed.

Chapter Seventeen
Sensing Your Way Deeper Without a GPS

When we realize that we can't trust our thoughts we're way ahead of the game. As Albert Einstein said, "I think 99 times and find nothing. I stop thinking, swim in silence and the truth comes to me." How interesting that Einstein here is describing the wordless openness to possibility that is essential to Zen practice. However, discovering that we can't trust our thoughts temporarily leaves us hanging in mid-air. If we can't trust our thoughts then how can we navigate life?

In a book called *Wayfinding* by M.R. O'Connor we can see how a Hawaiian named Nainoa Thompson, now famous for his traditional Hawaiian navigation skills, learned to go beyond thought. One night when the clouds obscured the moon and the water was too choppy to "read," Nainoa found himself lost in the middle of the ocean. With seemingly nothing to navigate by, he began to panic until he realized that he could "feel" the moon:

> That night, I learned there are levels of navigation that are realms of the spirit. Hawaiians call it na'au—knowing through your instincts, your feelings, rather than your mind or intellect. It's like the doors of knowledge open and you learn something new. But before the doors open you don't even know that such knowledge exists.[1]

This is the same sense or ability to sense that we are born with and that is so important in deepening our Zen practice. We can never think our way to Awakening. We can never think our way to the innate freedom that is there in all of us. We have to tune in as this man did to something beyond ordinary knowledge, beyond our usual

---

1 *Wayfinding*, M.R. O'Connor, St. Martin's Press, 2019, pg. 242.

cognitive misperceptions, and experience the felt-sense beyond words in our body.

There are two miscellaneous koans that express this potential, as Nainoa describes, of knowing through your instinct and feelings[2] rather than your mind or intellect. Working on these koans will help us open to this process of Unknowing. The first one states "It will guide you back to the village on a moonless night." The second similarly reads, "It will help you cross the river when the bridge is broken down." When we are able to connect with the inherent spaciousness of not knowing, we can see many doors of possibility opening where before, when we try to solve a problem by thinking, we may see no options, or the one option we do see is blocked. We may then attach to the one we do see and prevent ourselves from opening to all the alternative possibilities, many of which would be far more effective.

Helen Keller writes in her book *We Bereaved*,[3] "When one door of happiness closes, another opens; but often we look so long at the closed door that we do not see the one which has been opened for us." As we continue to utilize our ability to sense more deeply, we discover that the doors exist only in our own mind and, in actuality, if we don't limit ourselves through thought, there's a whole field of viable possibilities.[4]

In contrast to the deep sense of awareness that these koans point to, the first few paragraphs of *Wayfinding* describe a couple who drive from Denver, Colorado to Taos, New Mexico. The next morning they decided to visit a nearby hot spring. They put the address in their GPS, follow its directions down an increasingly narrow set of twists and turns on dirt roads, finally arriving at a cliff overlooking the Rio Grande gorge with no hot springs in sight. GPS, like the thought patterns in our intellect, rely on a fixed interpretation of an environment, is not in contact with the environment itself, and may not be accurate. To rely solely on the intellect is to confuse the two-dimensional map for the three-dimensional, rich experience of

---

2 I suspect that when Nainoa says "feelings" he's not referring to emotions.

3 *We Bereaved*, Helen Keller, 1929. This book has since been reprinted various times in newer editions.

4 Intuition can be easily contrived unless we are free enough to not be attached to a result. Zazen can bring about letting go to the point where our intuitions will not be manufactured but will be accurate.

the environment that the map only points to. In other words, we often rely on prescriptive thinking that projects a model onto the world in front of us rather than receiving the present, unfixed, often ambiguous, fluid and unmediated reality we directly experience. GPS does receive updates but it functions like someone who customarily only watches Fox News but then decides to only watch CNN. There's a kind of update here, but it's an update that still exchanges one ideological paradigm for another and gets no closer to Reality. This is akin to using only our intellect to find our way through life. We're not disdaining intellect here. It can be a useful tool, but to consider it the only way to solve a problem is to eliminate the much more powerful option of using that part of the mind that does not depend on words.

Mario Mantese once told me[5] that five months after he was stabbed in the heart and ended up in the hospital mute, paralyzed, and completely blind, he began to see light and dark. After a year he could see clearly. Our growing ability to tune in to what is beyond unfolds like that gradually and in greater and greater clarity.[6] The more we trust it and engage it, the broader and deeper we are able to access it. When I realized early on in my Zen practice that I really couldn't trust my thoughts, it seemed to leave me in a kayak without a paddle in the middle of one of the Great Lakes. But then remembering in my much younger years where I had a sense that there was something important beyond thought, I began to open more to that wordless search, which naturally took me into that realm of possibility. I realized as I got deeper into it that out of all the possibilities there was always one that stood out, and when I went in that direction it always worked whether it made rational sense or not. I had learned I didn't have to think my way through life, I could simply open to that place beyond thought. It was not long after that that I was passed on my breakthrough koan.

As one Zen student reported after a year of residential training at Mountain Gate,

---

[5] In a personal conversation with Mario who was visiting Sōgen-ji when I was in residence there in 1994.

[6] There is a book called *Focusing* by Eugene Gendlin that can help you open to that ability.

Deepening my Zen practice has been, like the biblical story of Saul becoming Paul, as if blinding scales are dropping from my eyes. In that story, Jesus appears to Saul and blinds him. Through suffering, Saul reconsiders his life path and effectively goes through a journey of rebirth signified by his name change to Paul. In the process of this metaphorical rebirth reptilian scales fall from Saul's eyes like the skin sloughed off a snake. Saul, now Paul, sees anew.

For me, the scales represent the thought patterns, habit patterns, cyclical fixations and obsessions that have circumscribed and limited my perception and thus my life to a very narrow vision. For example, I would get caught in an obsessive indecision about possible life directions and choices. This pattern, I think, came in part from a culture that demands we cling to a plan with a fixed outcome in a kind of perfectionism.

But more significantly, it also came in experiences of frequent traumatic moments in my childhood where I was physically held down in unsafe situations that demanded escape but from which I could not escape. Since I couldn't run to safety in those situations, the pattern of frantically considering whether I can escape to the right, left, front or back, only to remain trapped became imprinted in my psyche. As an adult, I've continued to replay this psychic imprint of feeling trapped in indecision and desperate to escape almost any situation I've found myself in, including residential Zen practice and sesshins.

The difference with sesshin, however, is that I have been given a space of safety with a supportive and compassionate sangha where I could begin to explore the desperate need to assess my life for escape routes rather than reacting to that desperate need. During sesshins, then, I began to become aware of a massive, painful, almost atmospheric darkness that resided in my mind and body. This darkness scared me terribly but I would feel into it as best I could, sometimes weeping then backing away from it fearful that it would take me over entirely.

In hindsight, I realize that every sesshin since my first one two years ago was an experiment in feeling a little more deeply into that root darkness. To have opened completely to it from the first sesshin would not have been possible for me. Even if it were, it would have been too overwhelming and perhaps damaging. Eventually, after feeling enough into this darkness I was able to open to it and feel it fully. It passed through my body and transformed into a kind of humming light that sent pleasant shivers up and down my spine, arms, and legs. What had once seemed like this impenetrable, horrible darkness and fear was all of sudden gone.

I believe this darkness was the subconscious root of the indecision I'd constantly suffered in my thoughts. Since passing that darkness, my thought pattern of indecision and escape has begun to fall away, again, like dead scales from my eyes. As these scales fall away, there is a sense of openness, of possibility, and of an authentic unfolding of life that I can more fully trust.

Being able to use both our intellect when appropriate as well as our ability to understand without the need for words allows our life to be open, flexible, rich, and fulfilling. There is always change despite the anxiety that that brings up for people. When we're not locked into a rigid structure defined by our society, culture, and authority figures, we are fluid enough to embrace change. But society demands that we lock ourselves into a narrow view of what would be acceptable and admired. I was shocked when some good friends of mine told a young Zen student that she needed to have a five-year plan and a ten-year plan. How could you know what your inclination is, what you'll be drawn to, what your karma might bring five or ten years from now and how you might change in the meantime? And yet our culture demands it as if it were not honorable to step outside that narrow set of largely unspoken rules and live your own karmic path.

When we do the extended outbreath deeply, forgetting ourselves, every cell in our body opens with greater and greater awareness. If we embrace it and trust it, we are able to recognize our own guide star, thus stepping out of those narrow confines of society's "rules." This doesn't mean that we have to go against society's dictums; it means we are free to respect them and live in accordance with those dictums if that is our path, but we are also free to choose a different, non-standard path. For example, if you're drawn to becoming a pediatrician, even though it's within the confines of an acceptable societal path, it's not against allowing yourself the freedom to choose that. If you are drawn to become a bohemian artist who lives outside of society's standard paths, that's fine too. It's not about rebelling but about living from a place of authentic internal freedom.

It's very important to learn to tune into that awareness because not only will it help your zazen, it will also help you in your life in general. How? We are well-trained in using our intellect to navigate life, but it can leave us stranded. It can lead us into frustration and dead-ends as well as a feeling of not being good enough. The analytical mind is not always helpful and unfortunately, with so many navigation tools that we now have, our GPS, Google Maps and so on, we tend to forget how to read our environment, note landmarks, and trust that we will get where we're going even if we make a wrong turn. According to the NIH (National Institute of Health),[7] "Whenever such systems assist with self-localization and path planning, they reduce human effort for navigating. Automated navigation assistance benefits navigation performance, but research seems to show that it negatively affects attention to environment properties, spatial knowledge acquisition, and retention of spatial information." Our life is much more three-dimensional when we trust our own instincts, and allow those instincts to grow and develop, recognizing that while some people have retained this innate

---

7   Website: https://www.ncbi.nlm.nih.gov/pmc/articles/PMC6374493/

ability, others have overlaid it with fixed ideas. In order to be able to trust our intuitions we have to be unattached enough that we aren't driven by those fixed ideas.

We may even forget how to read the body language of people we encounter, thus making both us and them vulnerable to misinterpretation and misunderstanding. When we depend on our screens to define reality, we don't learn how to interact appropriately and harmoniously with other human beings. This may be one of the causes of violence so prominent in the world today. If we can't tune in to another person, it's easy to misunderstand their intentions and get caught in defensive behavior as a result. Social media constantly feeds us arbitrary, often inaccurate information, not just about news and politics, but about one another.

There's been much concern recently about the rampant bullying, shaming, and other abusive behavior aimed especially at teenagers through that media. Unfortunately, this is so impactive that it has resulted in suicides among targeted people.[8] Screens tend to separate us from the richness of personal interaction. And it's this illusory separation of self from other that breeds paranoia and mistrust. Contrast this with the compassion and sense of connection that derives from the experience of oneness that can be achieved through zazen.

In the process of tuning in to your full body experience of breathing out over and over and over, you will open increasingly to that inborn ability to experience beyond the need for words. An old friend of mine who trained in Japan to become a Butoh[9] dancer once told me as part of his training he and the other dance students were blindfolded, taken out to the countryside in a pickup truck, and left there for several hours with the instruction to remain blindfolded and sense their environment and learn to move around without using their eyes. People blind from birth often navigate from that ability to be present with their environment and tune into its subtleties. In a study, investigators randomly placed cardboard boxes and other

---

8 As of this writing, according to various news sources, multiple school boards and many parents have been suing and are continuing to sue Meta and other major social media companies over the mental health related deaths of teens.

9 A Japanese form of modern dance in which one tunes into one's deeper senses and translates that sense into slow movements.

obstacles down a long hallway then watched to their amazement as a blind man walked quickly down the hallway avoiding all of those obstacles. Jacques Lusseyran who was blinded at age eight recognized that he could move freely around his environment without bumping into things only if he was not caught in frustration, anger, or jealousy.

Then there's the man who, blind from birth, was filmed easily and accurately riding a bicycle.

As a newborn, with no recognition that he was lacking sight, he quickly discovered that, by making a clicking noise with his tongue, he could understand and interact with his environment. Not being hindered by any self-image of being blind he was not limited in discovering unique ways to engage the world around him. And so he learned to do lots of things sighted people learn to do like riding a bike.

There are many more things we can also learn to do when we don't stop ourselves because of assumptions and fixed ideas, particularly about ourselves. If we believe in the narrow definition of an identity, we are severely limited. Jacques Lusseyran was once asked to visit a teenager his age who had just been blinded. When he went to the other teen's home, Jacques found him sitting morosely in a chair, afraid to move. The teen was clearly caught in an identity that was self-limiting in terms of alternatives to living dependent on sight. He was not yet aware of the fertile sense of Unknowing that Nainoa Thompson had recognized when he couldn't "read" the ocean or see the moon.

Again, all of us have this built in sensing ability. As we do regular Zen practice, we open more and more to that innate ability. As was said above, if you feel unable to do that, get a copy of Focusing by Eugene Gendlin; study it. If you're having difficulty opening to that sense you may have what was once a legitimate reason not to feel. That feeling, as was expressed by the Zen student quoted in this chapter, can keep you caught until you're willing to open to the feelings that provoked the shutting down. You may find resistance to doing so, but if you persist, as he did, you will gradually be able to open into a new and clearer realm of experiencing.

Appendices

Glossary

Awakening Awakening is, to one degree or another, opening to the innate, condition-less state of the mind. Gradations of awakening are *kensho* and *satori* and *enlightenment*. (See *kensho*, *satori*, and *enlightenment*.)

Bodhicitta The desire to come to awakening for the benefit of all beings, i.e., to relieve suffering.

Bodhisattva Vow To vow, for however long it takes (including lifetimes), to relieve suffering in the world. Suffering can be beneficial in the sense that if we're not attached to our suffering, but sincerely wish to be free of it, it can serve as significant motivation to become free.

Chan Chan means "meditation" in Chinese. Originally coming from the word "dhyana" in India and subsequently became "zen" in Japan and "seon" in Korea.

Daimyo Local rulers of regions in Japan. Although the term "daimyo" changed with the political ebb and flow in Japan over the centuries, the daimyo were always large landowners with powerful clout; essentially rulers of their domains. The daimyo of the Ikeda clan's Okayama domain, on the occasion of his father's death, donated his summer home to become a Zen Buddhist temple "for the repose of his father;" the descendants of the Ikeda clan still live in the area but no longer have any real power.

Densu The lead chanter.

Dokusan See *sanzen*.

Dukkha Often translated as "suffering," the sense of this term can range anywhere from mild discomfort to profound anguish. It is often likened to a wheel not running true on its axle.

Fusui At Sōgen-ji, the main housekeeper and attendant who would greet guests, serve them tea, and otherwise be in charge of the main building under the roshi.

Gai Tan Sitting platform located outside the zendo proper but still within the same building. This is where new participants first sit before being admitted to the zendo. It's also a place where anyone injured or who cannot easily bend their legs in one of the two prescribed zazen postures sits.

Genkan The "business" entrance to a Zen temple, normally situated next to the kitchen.

Han The heavy wooden block that is struck to announce different events (such as *teisho*) in a Zen temple.

Hekiganroku *Blue Cliff Record* is a collection of koans originally compiled in 1125 in Song China, and expanded into its present form by Chan master Yuanwu Keqin.

Hondo The very large structure that is normally used for ceremonies and chanting in a Zen temple.

Jikijitsu The person who sits at the head of the jikijitsu-tan in the zendo and leads the sittings (meditation periods), striking the clappers and kinhin bell to define the rounds (shorter periods) of the sittings. The jikijitsu is normally a senior, experienced practitioner.

Jisharyo The "keeper of the back door" is the other major position of the zendo. The jisharyo serves as the "mother" of the zendo, going to find people if they're not in the zendo on time, and takes care of anyone in the temple who is ill. The jisharyo is responsible for making sure people follow the rules. (When Mitra-roshi was first assigned the duty to be jisharyo at Sōgen-ji, having come from the

Glossary

Rochester Zen Center—which has a very different arrangement that does not include the term "jisharyo"—she asked Chi-san, "What does a jisharyo do?" Chi-san responded, "Makes sure everyone follows the rules." Mitra-roshi then asked, "What are the rules?" Chi-san answered, "You'll find out.") Among other duties, they take care of the altar, change the water offerings daily, and serve the tea and sweets every night during sesshin. The jisharyo's duties involve making the way smooth for people; in that category, they see that lights are turned on/off, doors are opened/closed, and messages are relayed from the teacher.

Katsu An ornamental stick, symbolizing the official rank of a roshi.

Keisaku Also known as the *kyosaku* in Soto, the keisaku is the "encouragement stick" that has come down to us from ancient times in China, normally used to center and re-energize meditators when they are struck on acupuncture points on the back of the shoulders. It is not used at Mountain Gate, nor at many other Zen centers, as even the sound of someone being struck can be triggering for one who has experienced trauma.

Keisu A bronze bowl of various different sizes struck as part of chanting services

Kensho Literally "seeing into." An experience of seeing into one's essential nature. While kensho is significant, there are deeper levels of awakening to our true nature including satori and, deeper than that, full *enlightenment.*

Kesa The formal outer robe of a Zen Buddhist monk.

Koan Originally: a public record or case. A Zen paradox, question, or episode from the past that defies logical explanation. Koans are sometimes thought of as Zen riddles, but this is not entirely accurate since most riddles are intended to be solved through reason. A student undertaking koan work is meant rather to exhaust the use of reason and conceptual understanding, and open to what comes before knowledge and thought, finally making an intuitive leap (see kensho). Koans today are used in the Rinai sect and the Rinzai-Soto combination sects, as well as the Soto sect, but in the first two they are employed differently than in the Soto sect.

Kosesshin A time of approximately seven hours a day for five to seven days of intensive Zen practice, generally with an extended work period in the mornings.

Kyosaku see *keisaku*.

Metta Loving kindness.

Mumonkan Also known as the *Gateless Gate*, a collection of koans compiled in the early 13th century by the Chinese Chan master Wumen Huikai during the Song dynasty.

Ni Female priest.

Osesshin The term used at Sōgen-ji, the Zen temple in Okayama, Japan, for a "big" sesshin, i.e., one that lasts seven days and has a full schedule of approximately twelve to fourteen hours of meditation each day.

Rohatsu (Rohatsu Sesshin) The most intensive sesshin in the Zen Buddhist practice calendar. It classically runs from Nov. 30th into December 8th, and commemorates the meditation retreat in which the Buddha attained complete Awakening. See *sesshin*.

Roshi In Rinzai Zen, this title refers to someone who has done decades of training under a recognized Zen master, and has completed a significant period of teaching under the auspices of that Zen master before being recognized as a senior teacher in their own right. The timetable for this process varies among Rinzai teaching centers, but a deep enough level of Awakening—authenticated by a recognized Zen master—is a prerequisite.

Saha The "Saha World" in Mahayana Buddhism refers to the mundane world other than nirvana.

Samsara The beginningless cycle of repeated birth, mundane existence, and dying over and over again.

Samu Work practice.

Sanzen In Rinzai, a formal, private meeting with an authorized teacher. During this meeting, the student is given specific guidance in their Zen practice. If a student is working on koans, it is where the student presents a demonstration of their understanding of the koan they are working on. These koan demonstrations will normally happen in multiple sanzens, sometimes for many years, before a student is permitted to move onto another koan. (One is never *fully* "passed" on a koan, as there is always deeper to go.)

Satori A deeper level of opening to our true nature than *kensho*.

Seiza One of the traditional postures in Japanese Zen. Employed with a "seiza bench," you kneel on the mat and place the bench behind you, and sit back.

Seon "Meditation" and the "meditation" sect ("Zen" in Japanese) in Korea.

Shogun The title of military rulers appointed by the emperor in Japan, spanning from 1185 to 1868.

Shoji Sliding panels that form the walls in traditional Japanese homes and temples. Those closing off the outside may or may not have glass panes. Interior shoji are typically light weight frames covered with Japanese rice paper.

Susok'kan Also known as the practice of extending the out-breath, is the preliminary and primary meditation practice taught in Rinzai Zen. It is normally continued as part of koan practice when the student is ready. One is normally taught to begin it by focusing on the experience of the extension of the outbreath, with normal pace for the in-breath. It is a very grounding practice, and can take one very deep if accompanied by a sense of openness to possibility that if one does the practice deeply enough, what we are consciously or subconsciously looking for through Zen practice will be revealed.

Taiko Japanese drums or the performance of Japanese drumming.

Tan The raised platform on which temple participants sit zazen. In the Soto sect the tan is narrow, only deep enough to hold a mat (zabuton) on which there is a sitting cushion (zafu). In Rinzai temples, it's deep enough to accommodate a futon, upon which the monks sleep at night.

Teisho The roshi's expression of the Dharma, usually given as a talk, sometimes on a classic text, sometimes on a koan, or sometimes as a different expression of the Dharma.

Tenzo The Japanese term for the head of the kitchen in a Buddhist temple or monastery in Japan.

Yaza "Night sitting." Yaza is informal sitting after any formal day of meditation. During formal sittings, all participants sit in assigned seats and for specifically timed meditation periods. During Yaza one can sit anywhere outside or inside and according to one's own sense of timing. It is a very powerful support for formal sitting.

Zafu We know these in English as "sitting cushions."

Glossary of *kanji* (Japanese Character) Translations

Chapter 1 定礎 (*teiso*) laying a foundation

Chapter 2 苦杯 (*kuhai*) bitter ordeal

Chapter 3 放す (*hanasu*) release, free

Chapter 4 答え (*kota*) answer to a question

Chapter 5 地獄 (*jigoku*) Hell

Chapter 6 限 (*gen*) limit, restrict

Chapter 7 錦 (*nishiki*) brocade

Chapter 8 生修行 (*sei shugyō*) life and discipline

Chapter 9 釈放 (*shakuhō*) release, liberation

Chapter 10 健闘 (*kentō*) good fight, strenuous efforts

Chapter 11 昭 (*shō*) luminous

Chapter 12 涅槃 (*Nehan*) Nirvana

Chapter 13 空虚 (*kūkyo*) emptiness, void, inanity

Chapter 14 流 (*nagasu*) flow of water

Chapter 15 利 (*ri*) advantage, benefit

Chapter 16 続 (*tsuzuku*) continue, follow, ensure

Chapter 17 下念 (*shita nen*) beneath thought-mind

Recommended Reading

A Bird in Flight Leaves No Trace: The Zen Teachings of Huangbo with a Modern Commentary
Edited by Seon Master Subul, translated by Robert E. Buswell Jr. and Seong-Uk Kim
Wisdom Publications, 2019

And There Was Light: The Extraordinary Memoir of a Blind Hero of the French Resistance in World War II
by Jacques Lusseyran
New World Library, 2014

The Bodhisattva's Embrace: Dispatches from Engaged Buddhism's Front Lines
by Alan Hozan Senauke
Clear View Press, 2010

The Cloud of Unknowing: And The Book of Privy Counseling
by author unknown
Shambhala, 2009

The Color Purple
by Alice Walker
Penguin Books, 1987

Complete Guide to the Buddhist Path
by Kenchen Konchog Gyaltshen
Snow Lion, 2010

The Complete Poetry & Prose of William Blake
by William Blake, edited by David Erdman
Anchor Books, 1982

The Discourse on the Inexhaustible Lamp
by Torei Enji
Shobo-an Zen Centre

The Enlightened Mind: An Anthology of Sacred Prose
Edited by Stephen Mitchell
Harper Collins, 1991

Focusing
by Eugene Gendlin
Bantam Books, 1978

Going on Being: Life at the Crossroads of Buddhism and Psychotherapy
by Mark Epstein
Wisdom Publications, 2009

The Hazy Moon of Enlightenment
by Taizan Maezumi Roshi and Bernie Glassman
Wisdom Publications, 2007

Two Zen Classics: Mumonkan & Hekiganroku
Translated with commentaries by Katsuki Sekida
Weatherhill, 1977

John Keats: The Complete Poems
by John Keats, edited by John Barnard
Penguin Classics, 1994

In Love with the World: A Monk's Travels Through the Bardos of Living and Dying
by Yongey Mingyur Rinpoche
Random House, 2021

Luminous Mind: The Way of the Buddha
by Kalu Rinpoche
Wisdom Publications, 1993

Recommended Reading

Poison Blossoms from a Thicket of Thorn
by Hakuin Zenji, translated by Norman Waddell
Counterpoint, 2017

The Record of Linji
Translation and commentary by Ruth Fuller Sasaki, edited by Thomas Yūhō Kirchner
University of Hawaii Press, 2008

Taking the Path of Zen
by Robert Aitken
North Point Press, 1982

Tales of the Dervishes
by Idries Shah
Ishk Book Service, 1982

Toward a Psychology of Awakening: Buddhism, Psychotherapy, and the Path of Personal and Spiritual Transformation
by John Welwood
Shambhala, 2002

The Undying Lamp of Zen
by Torei Enji, translated by Thomas Cleary
Shambhala, 2010

Wayfinding: The Science and Mystery of How Humans Navigate the World
by M.R. O'Connor
St. Martin's Griffin, 2019

We Bereaved
by Helen Keller
Isha Books, 2013

You are the Eyes of the World
by Longchenpa, translated by Kennard Lipman and Merrill Peterson
Snow Lion, 2011

The Zen of Living and Dying: A Practical and Spiritual Guide
by Philip Kapleau
Shambhala, 1998

Zen Mind, Beginner's Mind: Informal Talks on Zen Meditation and Practice
by Shunryū Suzuki
Weatherhill, 1970

The Zen Monastic Experience
by Robert Buswell
Princeton University Press, 1993

About the Author

Born eight months before the attack on Pearl Harbor plunged the United States into the Second World War, Mitra-roshi grew up with war, the threat of war and the threat of loss and violence always as a backdrop. With it came a pervasive sense of suffering—and the sense that there is something deep, profound and liberating that could be found in the midst of suffering, if she could only return to experiencing it. When her grandmother bought her a Bible for her tenth birthday, she studied it, determined to find that connection somewhere in those tissue paper thin, gold-edged pages. But it was too soon. Decades later after many years of intensive Zen practice, she would return to that book and find within it expressions of the light she sought.

On January 1, 1974, she found her true home in Rinzai Zen Buddhist practice, for it offered not only glimpses into that sense of something deeper she'd always had, but a set of tools—zazen, koan work, support for that essential wordless inner questioning—that could make possible that reconnection. After sitting zazen on her own for a year and a half, a deep spiritual experience brought her to seek more intensive training at the Rochester Zen Center. Following two sesshin [meditation retreats] she was accepted to residential training at the Center, and trained intensively under Roshi Philip Kapleau until he retired and moved to Florida in the late 1980's. She was ordained by him in 1986.

When Harada Shodo Roshi visited the Rochester Zen Center in 1991, she recognized a deep connection, and a friend gifted her a sesshin with him in the Northwest United States. A year later she attended a second sesshin with him there and continued on to spend three months in Japan, two of which were spent in residence at Sōgen-ji, Harada-roshi's training center in Okayama; this was followed by sitting with Morinaga Soko Roshi's Sangha at Daishu-in in Kyoto, and finally by attending the Rohatsu sesshin in Obama at Bukkoku-ji, under Harada Tangen Roshi, before returning to the Rochester Zen Center with the firm knowledge that she needed to return to Sōgen-ji to continue her Zen training. Several months later she did return, and trained intensively at Sōgen-ji and Tahoma Monastery, Harada-roshi's American monastery until Roshi Kapleau called her back to Rochester in 1996 to authorize her to teach. She then moved to New Mexico and established Mountain Gate-Sanmonji, [sanmonjizen.org] and concurrently was asked to take over as teacher at the Hidden Valley Zen Center (HVZC) in San Marcos, CA.

She also continued to return to Sōgen-ji for 5-6 weeks every year for the next fifteen years for additional training, and attended every sesshin in the U.S. taught by Harada Shodo. She divided her time as well between building Mountain Gate and teaching also at HVZC. About seven years ago Harada Roshi asked her to take on his senior student, Sozui Schubert, "and make her your successor." Over the next several years, working with Sozui, she established her as Sensei at HVZC. Mitra-roshi retired from her position as Spiritual Director there in 2020 to devote full time to teaching at Mountain Gate.

A natural outcome of her growing up during a period fraught with wars, in 2013, Mitra-roshi expanded the offerings at Mountain Gate from twelve 7-day sesshin a year to also include three to four special retreats, the RegainingBalance Retreats for Women Veterans with PTSD. Somehow in the midst of a very full teaching schedule, she still finds time to continue her deep connection with her family—her sons and their families, her grandchildren, and her great-grandchildren.

Fully convinced that spiritual longing is at the heart of all religions, and that the deepest Truth can be found regardless of religion, her teaching draws from the wellsprings of Buddhism, the teachings of Jesus and other Christian contemplatives including Meister Eckhart, Rumi and other Sufi saints, as well as other deep spiritual seekers. She continues to teach full time at Mountain Gate.

www.ingramcontent.com/pod-product-compliance
Lightning Source LLC
LaVergne TN
LVHW041539050125
800567LV00046B/1034